Dancing Naked Under the Moon

Uncovering the Wisdom Within

Mary Bea Sullivan

Printed in the United States of America.

Front cover design by Patrick Krohn.
Front cover artwork by Cathy Kiffney. Used by permission.

ISBN 13: 978-0-9815-460-7-0
ISBN 10: 0-9815460-7-2

This book is dedicated to

Malcolm, Brendan, and Kiki—your love inspires me

Erin and Daniel—yours are the smiles of hope

Endorsements

"I've often wondered what students take home with them from spiritual retreats. This beautifully written and beautifully honest account of one woman's journey of transformation gives me hope. With sincerity, commitment, and a sense of humor like Mary's, we can all get there! From her hard-earned experience, she shows us how even the tragedies and ordinary obstacles of life can become powerful catalysts to growth."
—Rev. Cynthia Bourgeault, director of The Aspen Wisdom School and author of The Wisdom Way of Knowing and Centering Prayer and Inner Awakening

"Mary Bea Sullivan's Dancing Naked Under the Moon is a compelling spiritual memoir of great simplicity and honesty. As she shares her story, you discover your own, and together you walk the unmarked path of awakening."
—Rabbi Rami Shapiro, author of Ethics of the Sages and The Sacred Art of Lovingkindness

"This is the story of a spiritual pilgrimage told with candor, passion, and humor, and it is a joy to read. Mary Sullivan is a high-energy person of finely-tuned sensibilities who has been attentive to her very modern life and its losses of a friend, a marriage, and a career, and also to the Spirit who has been speaking to her in all the events that are described in this readable narrative. All who care about the spiritual quest can benefit from reading this poetic and wise book."
—Dr. Fisher Humphreys, author of I Have Called You Friends and Thinking About God

"Mary has a very powerful and helpful story to share because of her varied experiences, especially in relation to other faiths. There are many, many women who will be touched and helped and supported by her telling her story so honestly. I found myself laughing and crying throughout the book. It was so very refreshing, her honesty....the swearing and drinking and the despair that she bravely

spoke about. I was reminded of Henri Nouwen's The Wounded Healer and Elizabeth Gilbert's Eat, Pray, Love."
—Caroline Humphreys, one of the founders of Contemplative Outreach in Birmingham, Alabama

"I was transfixed by Dancing Naked Under the Moon! My heart beat in sync with Mary on each page of her story of being swept off her charted course. In the midst of loss and grief, she summoned the courage to surrender her path and simply follow THE Path and trust Life to unfold. Its interweaving trails have led through suffering and shedding, seeking and serving, to surprise and celebration. The hope for Mary's readers lies not in tips for a straight-line, one-time trip from suffering to celebration but in a candid testimony about simply staying on the Path and allowing it to form us and lead us Home."
—Carol Padgett, PhD, author of the Keeping Hearth and Home Series

Table of Contents

Foreword by Wayne Muller ix

The Primitive Woman x

Introduction xiv

Catching Up xv

Why Write This Book? xvii

Part One: Losing 1

A Last Week with Rhonda • The Important Questions • Mother Mary's Comfort • Longing for a Faith Home • Beer and Cigarettes • Tibetan Prayers • Fear • Rhonda's Last Call • Lama's First Call

Part Two: Longing 19

Love Thy Neighbor • Wagon Magnolia • The Holy Spirit and Life Saver Necklaces • Swinging • Yuka's Kindness • Monday Meditations • Faith • Hope • Love • Shared Stories • Care Team Training • Unfurling • Circle

Part Three: Leaving 43

Breaking Vows • East-West School • Feeding the Monster • Being the Monster • Slow Burn • Truth Telling • You Should Go Home • Voices • Pushing the Boulder • Rocking Chair Revelation • Blazing a New Trail

Part Four: Finding 71

Naming Me • Who Would I Become? • Telling Family • Crystal Box • Out in Public • Riding Toward My Future • Piña Coladas • Sleepless

Part Five: Loving 89
Pastor, Mentor, Lover, Come Home, Come Home • Beginnings • Natural Disasters • Airport Pick-Up • Flying • Long-Distance Love • Running • Milkshakes

Part Six: Searching 105
Let Jesus in the Boat? • Remembering and Forgetting • Yankee Catholic Meets Southern Baptist • African Treasures • Interdependence Day • Emergency Room Insight • Scouting Home

Part Seven: Landing 131
Social Worker Wisdom • Sabbatical Guide • Consenting • Sabbath Walk • Brush Strokes • Peeling the Onion • Caroline's Gift • The Traveling Talking Stick

Part Eight: Healing 165
Broken Open • Power of Story • Healing Services • Pinch-hitting Preacher Hits Homerun • Weeding • Wisdom's Dance

Epilogue 183

Acknowledgements 185

Foreword

Santa Fe, January 2008

The story of any one woman is always unique, particular, private. But at the same moment any deep, aching unfolding of the heart and soul of any woman is deeply ordinary. Because it is always in the most ordinary of stories—of life and death, love and loss, brokenness and courage, confusion and wisdom—that we discover most frequently the regular appearances of the most extraordinary miracles. What is new cracks through the torn fabric of what we cannot bear to let go, the light shines through the cracks of our being well-used, the wellspring of our gifts pours out of us when we are knocked off-center and fall, without plan or reason, somehow pulled by the gravity of grace into the absolutely right next thing.

Women who tell the truth know these things. If they are friends or lovers, they learn and share these truths together.

Mary Sullivan's story is, as she confesses, quite ordinary. It is about love. And loss. It is about never walking away but always toward the fear, the sharp edges, the brambles, the sloppiness of intimacy, the ache of truth, the fall into unknowing faith. She shows us courage, despair, learning to pay attention, seedling faith, and the consequent inevitability of ordinary miracles.

Mary's journey begins with the aching loss of a beloved friend. But in what follows, she gently challenges us: What is it we take for granted in what we have, in who we become, in what we do, that seduces us into sleep, only to be awakened when we are broken open by the loss of everything?

As she bares her tender wounds, shares her unpredictable salvations, and maintains an infectious, holy curiosity about it all, Mary Sullivan offers the story of her inner pilgrimage not to lift up her own life, but rather as a gift, a companion, a kind of gentle nourishment, for ours.

I recommend you read what she has written, breathe it in, and offer whatever gratitude we offer anyone who has walked the dark before us and returned with the certain promise of light.

—Wayne Muller

author of Sabbath, How Then Shall We Live? and Learning to Pray

The Primitive Woman

Waiting for a friend in a favorite bookstore, I pulled out a notepad to write. "What makes my story unique?" I scribbled. Pen in mouth, pensively considering this important question, I continued, "In a way it isn't, because mine is a story that has been told and retold in various ways by women since the beginning of time." Imagining what it might have been like for the first woman who experienced a crisis of faith in the middle part of her life, I daydreamed. Then the pen began flying across the paper. This is what I wrote.

***

Primitive Woman is cooking meat stew, two toddlers clinging to her legs. She points for them to pick up the sticks they have been playing with, yet they refuse to obey her. Her mate, Man, is away hunting often and she frequently forgets his scent.

Survival requires that she surrender to the rules and rituals of the tribe. The tribe acknowledges the presence of a Great Spirit. Whenever they gather to honor, praise, and thank the Great Spirit, the men dance and the women watch. This practice is never questioned. Without much thought, day in and day out, Woman forages for plants, cooks her stew, picks up the sticks for her children, observes sacred ceremony, and shares a bed with her man when he comes home.

An unfamiliar and disturbing uneasiness creeps into Woman's heart. One particularly difficult day, to the children's surprise, to her man's surprise, and especially to her surprise, primitive woman bellows—a series of deep, angry, frustrated grunts come from the depths of her belly. Standing in front of the rough-hewn pot full of stew, she throws down her stirring stick, turns from the cave and walks off into the woods alone. Man and children alternate staring blankly at each other and the direction of the exiting woman. She is the center of their universe. Man worries, "Who will cook the stew?" The children wonder, "Who will take care of us?"

Woman's leaving reverberates throughout the tribe. When the women of the tribe notice she is missing, they cast wary looks toward the woods, wondering what called their sister away. The other men of the tribe are both smug that their woman didn't leave and concerned that it could happen to them.

Scared, alone, and confused, Woman walks until she can walk no more. It is nightfall. She has never slept away from the cave or the safety of her tribe. As the moon rises, she curls up in a ball and shivers on the cold ground in the woods. Cloaked only in the buffalo hide clothing her tribe prefers, she finally falls asleep. Later she is wakened by the howling of nearby wolves. Vulnerable and lost, she considers going back to the safety of the cave. She questions her choice to leave the tribe. Eventually, she drifts off again into a fitful sleep.

At daybreak, a glimmer of hope breaks through with the rays of sun. Woman decides to prepare for the coming night by building a small shelter using nearby branches. She gathers leaves to make a soft bed. Although she is still quite afraid, Woman sleeps much better the second night, inside the home she has created. Over the next few days, she survives by eating the berries and plants her mother taught her to gather long ago.

In the silence, Woman feels the constant presence of Great Spirit as never before. When the sun rises she feels Great Spirit as a warm protective blanket. When she drinks at the river her thirst is quenched by the essence of Great Spirit. The void created from voices left behind is replaced with the ever-present whisper of Great Spirit.

Eventually, Woman misses meat enough to attempt hunting. Try as she might, she cannot make her rudimentary spear go where she wills it. Determined and hungry she continues to hunt, with no success. One day she manages to kill a rabbit by waiting patiently in the bushes and stabbing it with her spear. Ravenous for meat, she immediately builds a fire, cooks and eats the rabbit. After numerous attempts, she tracks and kills an elk. Standing over her kill, one foot planted on its torso, her spear piercing the sky, Woman whoops out a victory cry.

That night under the full moon, Woman lights a fire. Examining the elk hide, she prepares it to be her cloak, a replacement for her traditional buffalo skin. Sitting by the fire, Woman cooks the meat and treasures the taste of her independence.

Satiated, Woman reclines near the fire and stares up at the moon. Turning an ear to the ground, she hears the beat of drums reverberating through the earth. Even after lifting her head from the ground the mysterious beat continues, now from within her; pounding, growing louder and more intense. Compelled by a desire to give form to this beat, she stands with her arms outstretched to the sky and begins to move. The confining feeling of the buffalo skin against her becomes unbearable and she flings it off into the fire, which blazes with its new fuel. Her heart drums with the beat and breaks open into oneness with ALL, something she has never experienced before. Her bare feet stomp out the beat of the drums until she finds herself whirling freely, dancing naked under the moon.

Exploding with gratitude, love, joy, and in communion with Great Spirit, Woman dances until her body glistens with sweat and aches with exhaustion. At daybreak, she climbs into her shelter to rest, knowing it is nearly time to return home.

Weeks later, feeling the primal pangs of loneliness, missing her children, man, and sisters, Woman prepares to leave her sanctuary. She enters the river and swims naked one last time, savoring the feel of the cool water upon her skin and the warmth of the sun upon her face; attempting to capture this feeling of oneness and power to take it back to the cave with her. Removing the elk hide from the enclosure she has created to smoke-cure it, she adorns herself with her new robe. The soft hide feels odd against skin that has become accustomed to being unencumbered, exposed. Leaving the woods, Woman begins the long trek home, the beat of her feet keeping step, footfall by footfall.

Weary from travel, Woman notices smoke rising in the distance and approaches her tribe. She pauses to lean on her walking stick. Nervous, but resolved, she enters at the height of the evening activity, regal in her robe. There is a hushed silence as all eyes gaze in her direction. The primitive woman has returned, but she is a different woman. Her children are overjoyed and immediately rush to her, stroking and admiring her new cloak. Primitive Man is intrigued and confused by this changed woman. Some of the sisters grunt and purposefully turn their backs, while others are drawn to this powerful new woman. Primitive woman is impervious to the judgments of others and without judgment of them. Her heart beats to the drum of the One Heart. For the first time in her life, she has found her own step dancing naked under the moon.

***

Resting my pen on the table, I gazed out the window at the cars lined up like crayons in a box. Here I was in this twenty-first century existence, yet something about primitive woman's story touched me deeply. Why? I wondered. This is what I wish for myself, I thought. No, this is what I wish for anyone desiring to make dramatic life changes—the courage to leave the conventions of their tribe and find their unique dance—the dance intended for them by Great Spirit.

Introduction

Seven years ago I lost the best friend I had ever had to breast cancer. Her name was Rhonda. The day her obstetrician told her the tumor was malignant, she was thirty-four years old, her daughter was three years old, and her son was three weeks old. Walking closely beside Rhonda as she struggled with cancer for five years was, for me, the beginning of a journey toward wholeness that continues today.

What I remember most about Rhonda is an abundance of laughter and a fascination with all things spiritual. The love she gave me was unique in my life. My courageous friend showed me how to swallow life whole, with open-hearted joy. She was my kindred spirit and confidante. When she died, my soul was torn and a gaping hole was left. It would take years and some dramatic choices to heal the wound from the inside out.

This great loss catapulted me into a period of painful questioning. Watching Rhonda lose her life made mine more valuable. I tormented myself about nearly every aspect of my classic suburban life. Basic choices were called into question, like staying married to my husband of sixteen years, leaving a career to be a stay-at-home mom, living in the standard four-bedroom-two-and-a-half-bath house. I wondered how my days had become so uninspired. I could no longer take time for granted and knew I wanted to make a difference in the world, but how?

My connection to the Divine was confused as well. I had traveled far from my Catholic roots and was not sure where I belonged. The biggest question that dogged me was this: Will my life really matter?

Saying good-bye to Rhonda marked the beginning of a series of major personal changes for me. With each new letting go, I peeled away another layer of the roles, beliefs, and conventions I had cloaked myself in for the first forty years of my life. Like the primitive woman whose story I told at the beginning of this book, I could no longer bear the feel of those garments against my skin. But if I wasn't those things, what was I? Who was I? Naked and scared, I set off to find out.

Catching Up

The story you are about to read begins in my thirty-seventh year. In an effort to "catch you up," as they say in the south, let me give you some glimpses of my life before our story begins.

I am the fifth of eight children; my Irish Catholic mother was pregnant ten times in twelve years. My German father was raised Lutheran, but after seven years of attending church with mom, he converted to Catholicism, inspired by mom's faith and for the sake of family unity. Growing up, I believed the words "Catholic" and "Christian" were synonymous. The fact that I missed all those other denominations doesn't say good things about my observational skills. Maybe I just thought Catholic was the right kind of Christian.

We moved around a lot for my father's job with Mobil Oil. Moving was easy for me, because mom did all the work. Besides, with such a large family, I brought my best friends with me wherever we went. I was luckier than my older and younger siblings—we stayed in the same place, Cherry Hill, New Jersey, from my sixth to twelfth grade years.

In Cherry Hill, I figured out there weren't only Christians in the world—there were also Jews. They threw the best parties when their kids turned thirteen. I envied my Jewish girlfriends with only one or two siblings. As a teenager, I didn't appreciate my loud, large family quite as much. Sometimes I saw my other siblings as competition for attention and for material things. Whenever I would lie in bed at night and imagine which brother or sister I wanted to get rid of, though, I felt compelled to confess it to the priest the next Saturday.

My handsome, popular brother Mike is two years older than me. When I was a senior in high school, Dad offered to fly me to visit him at the University of Dayton. Dad thought it would be nice for us to go to college together, and the fact that it was Catholic was a double bonus. I had no desire to go to the same college as my brother, but I changed my mind during the visit because the parties were wild and I fell in love. I enrolled for all the wrong reasons, graduated with a degree in finance, and at the ripe old age of twenty-two, married my college sweetheart, Van.

A year after we married, I was sitting in church one Sunday when something in me snapped, inexplicably. I was angry that women couldn't become priests. Who were these men making the rules, interpreting God's will? After years of being repressed and shushed, my inner rebel could no longer kneel quietly in the pew. She had to get out. She could not believe God saw women as inferior to men, and decided she couldn't worship in a church that saw her as a second-class citizen. It wasn't easy. I felt like I was betraying my heritage. If I wasn't a Catholic, what was I? How would I relate to God? To whom would I belong?

Besides walking out on organized religion, I spent most of my twenties working hard as a financial consultant, and playing hard at being what was then called DINKs—Double Income No Kids. I became so burned out that when my husband finished graduate school and was offered a job in Northern California, I couldn't run fast enough from the financial planning practice I had worked hard to build.

California…sunshine, babies, Rhonda. Rhonda and I first met when we were both working for a small telecommunications company. She was pregnant with Erin at the same time I was with Brendan. When I was forced to lie on the couch for weeks at the end of my pregnancy, Rhonda frequently called to check in on me. When the same thing happened to her a month later, I sent flowers, the card reading, "Hang in there! It's worth the wait."

When our babies were a few months old, Rhonda showed up unannounced at my back door. It was a beautiful Saturday afternoon in the fall. She had one arm around her baby, Erin, and the other holding out a bouquet of farmers' market flowers.

"I saw these sunflowers and thought of you," she beamed.

"That's so sweet, come on in. The house is trashed, but I'll make some tea." I was thrilled she had not called ahead. That's how our friendship was from then on—simple, spontaneous, with easy understanding. Rhonda gave me more freedom to be myself than anyone ever had. When I was with her, I knew who I was, and I knew that was good.

Thirteen months after Brendan was born, our daughter Kristin arrived. Brother and sister's first encounter was videotaped. I was sitting in a rocking chair in the hospital holding one-day-old Kristin. Toddler Brendan came ambling toward us and in a loving, slightly domineering kind of way, he began to pat (okay, hit) Kristin's head as he cooed, "Kiki. Kiki." The name stuck.

Neither Rhonda nor I was affiliated with any formal religion. Attitudes in California were open-minded, free-thinking, and free-wheeling. We were consumed with a mutual interest in all things spiritual—conventional church services were less common for us than tarot readings, energy healing, or chanting in Hindu with an Ayurvedic master. Underneath our seeking was a desire to connect with the Sacred—to know our lives had meaning.

When Erin was three, Rhonda's son Daniel was born. When her breast cancer diagnosis came a few weeks later, it added a new sense of urgency to our spiritual seeking. Living in the Bay Area, Rhonda had access to fabulous conventional and alternative practitioners.

When my husband and I decided managing two careers and two small children was too much, I joyfully offered to be the one to jump off the merry-go-round to stay home full-time. This opened the door for my husband to pursue a temporary overseas assignment. We thought Rhonda was in remission. When Van asked if there were any places in particular I wanted to live, I said just about anywhere, as long as it wasn't Asia. Soon after, he came home grinning. "Guess what? There's an opening in Tokyo!" The Jersey girl in me wanted to say, "Yo! What part of 'anywhere but Asia' don't you understand?" But I didn't. I did what my mother did, and her mother before her: I called the movers.

Tokyo…busy, scary, adventurous. Living in a Buddhist country opened me to meditation, yoga, and further exploration of many traditions. Practicing Eastern meditation and yoga, I experienced moments of peace which seemed most like what it would be to know "God." I was hooked. Although both Van and I were deepening our spirituality, our marriage suffered from the stress of living in a foreign land and his frequent travel.

Two years later we returned to California, and Rhonda's cancer also returned. She faced it with a deepened sense of acceptance some days, and a panicked desire to find the right cure others. Miraculously, she returned from the brink of death over and over with a renewed vibrancy and faith.

Hoping it would heal our bruised marriage, Van and I decided to relocate to Chapel Hill, North Carolina, in order to simplify our lives and be closer to extended family. Leaving Rhonda broke my heart, but I took for granted her ability to travel and her gift for healing. I was wrong on both counts. Shortly after I moved, Rhonda was told the cancer had metastasized to her brain. In a bold stroke that defied reason, six months before she died, Rhonda and her family moved closer to her beloved brother, to a place she longed to return to—Grand Junction, Colorado.

That is where this story begins, near the end of Rhonda's life and at the beginning of cataclysmic changes in my own.

Why Write This Book?

My story is unique, yet it is universal to all who have experienced a wake-up call that made them question and walk away from a life they have built. I invite anyone who is finding it harder and harder to exist in a life that lacks heart and meaning to take this journey with me. Your path may not be the same as mine, but I can testify that there is great joy in seeking out and finding your unique path.

This is the story of a spiritual quest—but perhaps all quests are spiritual. In this quest, I have melded traditional and non-traditional routes to the Sacred, finding value in both. This is a story of questions, not tidy answers.

It would be inaccurate to say this journey is only about

losing and leaving; because it is as much about finding and loving, in all its glorious messiness—loving myself, as imperfect as I am; loving my children, as imperfect they are; and loving those who are different from me, as imperfect as they are. Oh and yes, this is also a story of finding new love that I wouldn't have dreamed possible.

As I write this book some seven years after Rhonda died, my life is significantly different than when I was thirty-seven. The desire to write my story came to me during a sabbatical. Alone with my dogs and cat most of the day, surrounded by natural beauty, I found silence. The breath of God replaced the voices I left behind. Unfortunately, the solitude also created space for those pesky demons of anger, resentment, and fear—I could no longer run from them. At times, wisdom emerged from the silence. I was free from the binding daily conventions that both order and limit our lives. There were days when the glimmer of who I am shone through like the sparkles on the lake that surrounded me. Forgiveness also made an appearance now and then. I began to feel a renewed sense of purpose and restored hope during the peace of those days. Silence planted the seed for this book.

I never intended to share my journey. However, near the end of my sabbatical I realized that others who are facing similar roads might find comfort in my experiences—those who have lost a loved one, or a marriage, or struggled with their faith. I knew writing would help heal my wounds. I hoped it would be healing for others as well. I underestimated the powerful impact telling my story would have on me. Sometimes it was comforting to relive important events, other times it was greatly disturbing.

Writing this book feels like flashing in Times Square. Time and again while writing this book I have thought about putting a more positive spin on my life, my choices, and my mistakes. I wanted to hide my craziness and anger from you, my readers. I wanted you to like me, but I was afraid if you really knew me you wouldn't. I wanted you to think I was perfect. I wanted to hide my true beliefs for fear they would offend you or you would judge me.

But the primitive woman in me wouldn't settle for an insincere memoir filled with self-serving lies. She knew that the weight of wearing the wrong garment prevents us from dancing freely. She insisted that I be honest, so she could call her sisters out. My greatest hope is you will be emboldened to set your own primitive woman free.

In Dance of the Dissident Daughter, Sue Monk Kidd says, “To reconnect with our souls we need to claim the freedom and power to shed our conditioning, to tear out the stitches from the old fabric, and to define for ourselves who we are as women, what is sacred, and how we relate to sacred experience. When we finally do that, we will weave new lives and a new era. We will take back our souls once and for all.” This book is about taking back my soul and an invitation to any who wish to reclaim their own.

Of course, my journey continues. I know you, the reader, have your own unique journey to follow. Though our paths will certainly have differences, I believe we may also share some things in common. I believe that underneath labels like Jewish, Christian, Muslim, Taoist, Buddhist, and Hindu there is a universal longing to return HOME; and at our best, we embody the Hindu greeting namaste, which means “The divinity in me recognizes the divinity in you.” I hope that our spirits will recognize each other in the pages of this book. I hope that some of the trials, mistakes, and joys that I have experienced will be of value to you. Thank you for including me in your travels.

Namaste,
Mary Bea Sullivan

Part One: Losing

"One day you will have to solve an unbearable loss.... That is the way home.... Healing comes from the steps...."
—Anne Lamott

A Last Week with Rhonda

On Sunday, I crawled into bed next to my kindred spirit, Rhonda. We rested side by side with our opposing needs—Rhonda with her need for me to let her go, me with my need for more of her; more love, more laughter, more tears, more of everything. Selfishly I wondered, "After she dies, how am I supposed to go on?" How would any of us go on? She had deeply touched so many lives with her loving, living, and dying. How would we honor the gifts she had given us and keep on going?

Before her diagnosis, Rhonda had the taut physique of a runner. Now cancer and lack of exercise had eaten away so much of her that it was easy for both of us to fit into her hospital bed. Monitors beeped, tubes protruded, medicinal smells accosted my nose. All of my senses were offended by the scene in the hospital room. An oxygen tube was stuck up her nose, her color was grey, and her chest heaved deeply with every breath. Rhonda hadn't walked in more than a month and her ability to move her right side was minimal. Periodically a TV-like screen beeped if one of her vital signs dropped significantly.

Now we were lying in her bed together and the beeping had become white noise. I propped myself up on one elbow, trying to protect this new size two Rhonda from my size ten body.

"I'm okay, Mary. You can relax."

"Sorry. I know how you hate to be treated like someone who is sick." I snuggled in closer and stroked the thin wisps of her short hair. How many times had she surrendered her thick, light brown mane to this disease? How much had her family sacrificed at the altar of cancer? The final sacrifice impatiently lurked in the room, waiting to snatch her away.

Dancing the timeless dance of final conversations, we laughed, we cried, and we reminisced. We retold stories of time alone, without kids or husbands, of all of those "last chance" girls-only weekends we finagled because her prognosis seemed grim.

"Mary, thank you for loving Erin and Daniel."

"It's easy," I said as we locked wet eyes, knowing the two people most devastated by Rhonda's disease were her children, eight-year-old Erin and five-year-old Daniel.

"Rhonda, seriously, you've shown me how to live. I've never met anyone like you before. Thank you for teaching me what it means to be alive. Even in this hospital bed, you are more alive than most people I know who are healthy."

I was imploring her to understand what a gift she was to everyone who was connected to her. She seemed to take her indomitable spirit for granted. While I had the chance, I wanted her to know her living inspired me, changed me. "Remember the time you called for the kids and me to join you at the Christmas parade and I said I was too tired? When I hung up the phone I realized you had just returned from chemo. I felt like such a schmuck! I vowed after that not to miss the moments. Not just with you, but with everyone. Thank you."

She held my hand and stroked it with her thumb as she stared out the window, retrieving unseen memories from the mountains in her view.

"It all seems like yesterday." Rhonda whispered.

"And forever ago." After a long period of stillness, Rhonda asked for some water.

"Well, I know one thing I'm going to miss." I blurted out. "Nobody can swear as well as you can. Girl, you make a word like *fuck* sound so sophisticated. I'm going to miss that."

Rhonda almost spit out the water she was drinking from the cup I was holding for her. We giggled for a few minutes, enjoying the laughter that came easily. Then serene silence blanketed us; that came easily too.

The world inside her hospital room was small. We knew there were few new stories to create, so we held on to the old ones. Reliving them made us both feel more alive. I wanted desperately to make her world bigger again. She had lived large, outwitting the angel of death many times; I had come to expect it of her. But this time was different. I couldn't assume we would have more time. Hell, I didn't even know if she had the rest of the day.

"We had a lot of great talks on that patio of yours," I said, remembering the magical feeling of so many evenings, drinking wine while the kids played. It seemed like another lifetime, far from beeping machines and medicinal smells.

"I guess we were lucky we lived so close when the kids were little," Rhonda groaned as she tried to shift position.

Instinctively I moved toward her, but she repeated, "I'm okay." It must have taken great patience for her to train me. Every time she sighed or winced I wanted to wave some kind of healing wand and take away the discomfort I knew she was feeling. She kept pushing that morphine drip, had a fentanyl patch on her arm, and yet nothing could make it easier for her to breathe, nothing could take it all away. I felt so helpless. When I hovered over her too much, her independent spirit was insulted. I eventually surrendered, acknowledging that the only thing I offered that she seemed to need was my presence. My panic-to-peace ratio was improving.

Even though—perhaps because—we could smell death breathing down our necks, a presence of love and clarity pervaded that hospital room. For an entire week, we had been given plenty of time alone during the day so Rhonda's husband, Bill, and her parents, Bob and Anita, could have a break. For more than a month they had been working, tending to Erin and Daniel's needs, and holding a 24-hour-vigil by Rhonda's side.

I was spending every day of my week-long visit with Rhonda, and one of the other three caregivers would spend the night with her. The 24/7 companion duty was necessary because formerly fearless Rhonda was afraid. Her swallow reflex was weak and sometimes she would gasp, trying to clear the phlegm from her throat. After all the treatments and surgeries she had endured, Rhonda was afraid of choking. She knew she was going to die; she just didn't want to die choking and alone.

After a little while, Rhonda grimaced and asked me to pull her up higher in the bed. She said, "I loved those gorgeous Northern California days we spent playing at parks when the kids were little. Things were so simple then."

I climbed out of the bed and hooked my hands under her armpits, slid her up to the top of the bed, and then pulled the thin, white hospital blanket over her frail body.

"You picked a hell of a weight-loss program, girl!"

"Thank you for everything Mary—everything," Rhonda said with a sense of urgency. Tears welled up again in our eyes. I climbed back into bed, grabbed the brush resting on the table next to her bed, and began to brush what was left of her hair. Looking up at me with tenderness she whispered, "You must have been my mommy in another lifetime."

I leaned over and kissed the top of her head, love and sadness welling up inside me. How this gorgeous woman had opened me to life! How different I would be if we hadn't crossed paths. Thank God we had. All the love and laughter was worth the pain of losing her; in fact without it, there wouldn't be that pain.

"I'm not sure I've always been such a great friend. There were a few times when I really thought you were making some big mistakes—like the yoga retreat on the north coast."

She was beginning to doze off.

"It probably was crazy for me to go, but I'm glad I did," Rhonda muttered.

Her eyelids fluttered and she drifted off to sleep. "Me too," I thought. I watched Rhonda's face for a while and stroked her hair. Her beautiful skin was gaunt and ashen. Mostly she looked peaceful, but now and then her face would tighten up in a grimace and then release. My stomach ached with a gnawing sadness that wouldn't relent.

While she rested, I slid out of the bed, the stiff, starched sheets scratching my skin. I flopped into the blue vinyl recliner set by the window.

The Important Questions

Looking at her tiny form in the bed, I remembered our trip to the Northern California coast two years before. I had planned to attend a spring weekend yoga retreat with my teacher, Sara, at a rustic retreat center in the woods. When Rhonda heard about my plans she insisted, "I want to go too!"

I was taken aback. She hadn't been feeling at all well. I couldn't figure out how she would do yoga with a tube coming from her chest, connected to a pump feeding medicine into her body. But I kept silent about my reservations when Rhonda registered for the retreat.

A few weeks later we were driving through Sonoma County, lapping up the ever-changing scenery. Turning off Highway 101 and heading west toward the coast, we marveled at the rolling hills dotted with California oaks and the picturesque wineries of the Russian River valley. Farther down the road, we were enveloped by towering redwoods and lush forests. With each turn toward the coast, we turned away from thoughts of home. Windows down, we blasted Kenny Loggins and belted out, "PLEEEASE celebrate me home…" and then "Whenever I call you friend… now I know my life has given me more than memories, day by day…we can see…in every moment there's a reason to carry on…."

By the time we had driven the three hours to the retreat center, we were completely removed from mom mode and engrossed in girlfriend mode. On the first night, we sat in our cabin and pulled out Rhonda's tarot cards. Before placing the cards on the bed, Rhonda crossed her legs and closed her eyes, inhaling and exhaling deeply. I did the same.

"Okay, Mary what's your question?" Rhonda had asked as she opened her eyes.

"Will moving away from California help Van and me stay together?" I asked immediately.

For the past four years, I had been feeling restless in my marriage. I couldn't put my finger on what would make a difference, but I was often sad and resentful. During one of my trips home from Tokyo, I had considered staying in California with the kids leaving Van in Tokyo, alone. It took Rhonda, who was probably afraid that I would move in with her, and a psychic, who assured me there was "great adventure awaiting my return to Japan," to talk me into getting on the plane. Van had seemed unhappy for a long time as well. In our quest to reconnect, we wanted to make a significant lifestyle change. I wondered if moving away from the expensive, crowded California life to Chapel Hill, North Carolina, would help, or if it would be more of the same. This "feeling" had followed me from Ohio to California to Tokyo and back to California again. Was location really the problem?

Rhonda flashed a knowing look and flipped one card at a time face up on the brown-and-orange-striped comforter. Sitting across from her I listened as she interpreted the meaning of each card. I have no memory of her reading of the cards. I do remember laughing so hard I fell off of the bed when she looked me square in the eye and said, "Men! What we girls won't do to ride the big one!"

Next it was her turn. The mood turned somber.

"I want to know if I'm going to heal from this cancer. I know the doctors think it's grim right now, but I have so much more I want to do with my life." Her voice full of emotion, Rhonda absently swiped at a tear that had escaped to her cheek. "I wish I knew how much time I have left. You know, I go to one healer and he'll say, 'This breast cancer is due to a deep wound in your childhood. Heal the wound and the cancer will go away.'"

Pumping with indignation, she waved her arms dramatically.

"Another will say, 'More chemo, more surgery,' or 'Wear black hats to stunt the growth of the tumors.' Others want me to be realistic and 'Get your house in order.' I keep trying to stay connected to Spirit so I can know what truth is and what bullshit is." Then dropping her head and resting her cheeks on her palms, she sighed, "There is so much coming at me all the time, I don't know what I believe anymore."

I don't remember the outcome of Rhonda's reading, either. I do remember we both gave voice to fears of death: Rhonda about her physical death, me, the death of my marriage. Letting my fears escape and run around in the open was freeing and frightful. One of the greatest gifts of our friendship was the easy ability we had to share our hearts' deepest questions with each other—unfiltered, terrifying, and very precious.

The next morning when the yoga started, I still wasn't sure how Rhonda would participate. I felt a little self conscious that I had invited her, since she was sick. I was feeling responsible and worried that Sara would have to modify the class too much for a sick person. Later, when my courageous friend was asleep in her hospital bed, it turned my stomach to know I had let what others think bother me; that I had cared more about my standing with the yogis than I did about being with Rhonda.

While she was in down dog pose, Rhonda's pump came loose from her pants and fell to the floor with a bang. She simply picked it up and slipped it back in her pocket. Jamming my heels down into the mat, sticking my butt up high in the air, I was striving to have the best down dog posture in the class. Rhonda, meanwhile, retrieved her unruly pump as needed and gracefully rested when she was tired.

At the end of the two-hour class, Sara invited us to try partner poses. She instructed Rhonda to kneel with her head on the mat in child's pose. Then, I draped my body over Rhonda's with my back arched against the curve of her spine. My legs were stretched out in front of me and I lifted my arms overhead. As I leaned against her back I worried that my weight would be too much for her to hold. Gently, Rhonda clasped her hands around my wrists and pulled my arms, stretching my back. Her body seemed to say, "Lean into me. I will support you." We lay there silently, symbiotically, for a few moments. I surrendered my body fully. Breathing as one with her, I melted into blissful relaxation.

After a few minutes, Sara instructed Rhonda to slowly sit up and push me up, our backs against each other. Finally, we sat facing opposite directions, butt to butt, back to back, head resting against head. Seamlessly, we switched positions and I knelt in child's pose. Rhonda draped her body over mine, and I gently pulled her arms. The weight of her body on mine helped release the tension in my lower back. All the pairs in the room were quietly performing the same magical dance of giving/receiving, giving/receiving.

I had learned that the goal of yoga is to unite oneself with God; the practice of yoga is a path we can take to accomplish this. Peacefully surrendering my weight onto Rhonda's back, supporting her body, silently breathing as one with her, I had a glimpse of the true meaning of yoga.

Two days of immersion into conscious breathing and conscious movement helped me let go some of my competitive compulsion. As the weekend wore on, I was able to break free of a few of the chains of "doing it right."

Our yoga classes ended with students and teachers sitting cross-legged, palms together at the heart, bowing to each other and softly saying, "*Namaste*." During the closing session, I felt a sense of reverence for the sacred. I wanted to capture it in a bottle like a firefly and bring home with me. But I knew that, like a firefly, reverence needs air to breathe and space to fly. All these things ran through my mind that Monday in the hospital with Rhonda.

Mother Mary's Comfort

On Tuesday, tired and in pain, Rhonda didn't have the strength to open the little drawer of her bedside table. She was lying on her side with her head propped up on pillows. She wanted to pull out her rosary beads. "Will you get them for me?" she asked. Although Rhonda was not Catholic, a family friend had sent her the light pink strand of rosary beads. I reached into the drawer and found the beads.

"Do you remember how to say the rosary?" she asked. I thought back to when I was a little girl, praying the rosary with my parents and seven siblings.

"I think you say Hail Marys when you hold the little beads and Our Fathers on the big beads."

"That'll do," Rhonda whispered.

I leaned over her and placed a bead between her thumb and first finger. Softly I chanted the prayers, "Hail, Mary, full of grace…the Lord is with thee…." I slid a bead through her weak fingers after each prayer. The rhythmic chanting seemed to soothe her and take her mind off the pain. "Now, and at the hour of our death." I was surprised to feel comforted by this ritual, which until this moment had been long lost to me.

Rhonda closed her eyes. As I watched my friend rest, I became aware again of her radiant internal beauty. Those of us who knew her were drawn in by her sincere interest, care, and concern for us. To be loved by Rhonda was to be spoiled. She knew what you might want or need in a given moment, and she gave it.

I thought of the countless times that a nurse, respiratory therapist, or candy striper had entered Rhonda's room, expecting to be the caregiver. Despite her relentless pain and daily loss of function, Rhonda would turn the care around, and ask them questions.

"Give me the scoop—what's going on in your life?"

She listened intently to their answers, their stories, always wanting more information, details. And she never forgot anybody. Visitors and caregivers would leave her room feeling better than when they had entered. Oftentimes it was difficult to tell who was healing whom.

I was exhausted from lack of sleep and stress, and when I thought she was asleep, I started to remove the beads from her hand. Eyes still shut, Rhonda whispered, "Keep going."

I bent over her again and resumed the prayers. Every time I assumed she was asleep and attempted to stop, she would urge me, in a whisper, to "keep going." Finally, the pain subsided long enough for her to fall asleep.

Sometimes I was confused about my role with her during these days in the hospital. Should I cheer her up? Should I help her let go? Should I be quiet? Should I talk? Should I laugh? Should I cry? Should I stay? Should I leave? There is no rule book for being with the dying. All I knew was that I felt a deep sadness, deeper than anything I had ever felt before. I felt exhausted, heavy, and foggy. Ultimately, Rhonda was teaching me how to do this—how to be with her as she died. She was showing me how to drop my agenda and be with her at *her* pace. "Keep going," she had told me, over the rosary. "Don't stop. This quiet ritual soothes me. Stay. Keep doing what you're doing."

Longing for a Faith Home

Wednesday evening, when I returned to my hotel room after a day at the hospital, I flopped down on the bed exhausted, wishing I had a faith tradition to fall back on. Maybe praying the rosary with Rhonda had triggered my longing.

I had spent my twenties bouncing from church to church. Eventually, I visited the Lafayette-Orinda Presbyterian Church (LOPC) in Northern California. I watched as an impressive choir and parade of ministers made their entry into the large, formal church. The last minister in the procession was a young, pregnant *woman*. Rev. Rebecca Kuiken marched down the aisle with her short, red hair, broad smile, fertile belly, and aura of confidence. Electrical currents pulsed in my veins. My throat closed up and I tried to fight back the tears that were spontaneously flowing down my cheeks.

I was twenty-seven years old and this was the first time I had ever seen a woman in clergy robes. The vision of this wingless angel, in her white robes trimmed in gold, stole the air from my lungs. In that instant I found permission to redefine my role as a woman of faith. Witnessing Rev. Kuiken "owning" her place of honor, I knew that I no longer needed to feel like a second-class citizen; I would never participate in a faith community that marginalized women. From that first Sunday until we moved away from the area, I continued to attend LOPC, and Brendan and Kiki were baptized there.

When we moved, I stopped going to churches completely. It's hard to find women in the pulpit, and I was weary of being "preached to." I wasn't sure the priests or ministers were any better at navigating the waters of the human condition than I was. It seemed that I needed to take a break from organized religion so that I could explore a more personal relationship with the Sacred. I needed silence from doctrine so I could hear whispers from my heart. During this time of questioning, there was always a desire, a need, a yearning for connection to the Creator. This desire, this need, this yearning, transcended any religion. Years later, as I was facing the loss of my best friend, I was still questioning, still lost.

Tibetan Prayers

Thursday when I walked in the hospital room, Rhonda gave me an uncharacteristically serious greeting, her mood resigned.

"What is that Tibetan Buddhist prayer you told me about that is said for people while they are dying?" she asked.

Taken aback by the question, I thought for a few minutes, trying to remember what I had read in Sogyal Rinpoche's *Tibetan Book of Living and Dying*. I recalled something about the intention to pray for the soul as it passed from this life to the next, easing the transition. The details were foggy.

Finally I responded, "I'm not sure what it is called, I think it might be called *phowa*. Why?"

"Will you ask your sister Kathy to have her Buddhist friends say that for me when I die?" There was nothing morose in her voice, only surrender.

I tried to match her no-nonsense tone, "Sure."

"Hey, and while you're at it, make sure Anne has those people at the Tao Temple do their thing and your mom could say the rosary."

"Well, you've got all your bases covered, don't you?" I said.

Over the years, we had explored many different spiritual paths, books, and ceremonies together, sharing a keen interest in the world's wisdom traditions. It made sense that Rhonda would want to approach her death from this same inclusive perspective. She was fascinated by the fact that my siblings and I had chosen many diverse paths to the Sacred. I had told Rhonda about visiting with my sister Kathy after not seeing her for nearly a year. I noticed something new in Kathy. She was softer, happier. Her light blue eyes were more loving. When I told her, she said, "I've been taking teachings from a Tibetan Buddhist Nun, chanting, and meditating on a daily basis."

"Whatever it is you've got, I want it," I had said.

Rhonda had been intrigued by Kathy's transformation. Also the Buddhist teachings on impermanence and "not being attached to the outcome" had become part of her personal creed. Perhaps now that her own impermanence was impossible to escape, she found even more solace in those teachings.

Rhonda stared at the ceiling. "I'm ready to have someone bring up my jewelry and things so I can figure out where I want them to go," she said, her voice soft and peaceful.

Beer and Cigarettes

At the end of that emotional day, I lounged on the too-soft hotel room bed and felt a weird mix of exhausted and keyed-up. Sleep wasn't happening. In the midst of my biggest personal crisis, I ached for a spiritual home, a lifeline from God. Desperate, I left the hotel room, drove to a convenience store, and did something I hadn't done for a while. I bought a pack of Virginia Slim Lights, and for good measure, a six-pack of beer. Why would watching my friend dying of cancer make me want to smoke? How did I think filling my lungs with poison would bring me closer to the Almighty? I have no idea; there is nothing rational about terror or grief.

I shivered on the patio of my hotel room, raising the cigarette to my lips and sucking in the smoke, a reprieve from reality. Feeling a familiar rebelliousness, I smoked as many cigarettes as my body could stand, drank Coronas until I felt bloated. Lungs screaming from the frigid Colorado air and unaccustomed to nicotine, I slipped back into my hotel room, took a shower to rinse off the gritty, smoky stench and fell into bed, drained. Eventually sleep swallowed me, but I awoke exhausted.

Fear

Saturday, the day I was scheduled to fly back home, I didn't know what to do with myself. I was unsettled in Rhonda's hospital room and unsure of what to say. After days of effortless sharing, I was at a loss for words, nervous. Earlier that day, I had positioned myself farther away from Rhonda's bed under the auspices of not giving her the cold I had caught, probably the result of stress, smoking, and sleepless nights. Adept at moving from state to state or even out of the country, I didn't know how to say this kind of good-bye. Anita came into the room to relieve me so I could drive to the airport. When I stood up to go, a wave of vertigo struck me. I turned to Anita, feeling nauseous.

"I'm afraid to hug her because I'm sick," I lied. What I should have said was, "I'm afraid to hug her because I don't ever want to let her go."

No one said, "Go ahead hug her," or "perhaps you should keep your distance."

The choice was mine. I chose fear. I was trying to protect all of us from my pain. Rhonda knew me so well, if I held her she would know my heart was breaking apart. I didn't want her feeling responsible for my pain. I couldn't stand the emotions I was feeling. It all happened so fast and it seemed as if time stood in suspension, waiting for me to decide. Afraid to hurt her, afraid to say "good-bye," I looked into Rhonda's eyes for the last time, hoping my eyes could say what I seemed incapable of verbalizing. She smiled, tears streaking her face. The heaviness in my chest made breathing difficult.

"Thank you so much for coming," and then a bit breathless Rhonda added, "Thank Van for taking care of the kids so you could be here."

I tried to coat my broken heart with freon so I could walk out that hospital room door. How do you walk away from someone you love when they know it will be the last time? How do you say that good-bye?

I gave Anita what I couldn't bear to give her daughter, a hug. I reached for the metal handle on the wooden door, feeling numb and nauseous all at once. Hesitating, I pulled the cold piece of metal back and walked out the door, hearing the sterile click as it shut behind me. I couldn't imagine another door opening after I closed this one. I stood still in the shiny hospital hall, wanting more than anything to turn around and throw my body at the door, wailing.

Instead, I continued down the corridor and hugged good-bye to the nurses who had become my family for the week. I pretty much hugged everyone except the one person I needed to hug the most. The drive to the airport and the three plane rides it took to reach North Carolina were a blur of dark despair.

Rhonda's Last Call

A shrill ring pierced the quiet in our home on a Friday evening. It was Bob. He was at Rhonda's bedside; his voice was strained, but calm. Bob told me that he and the family were all there with Rhonda. She was too weak to talk on the phone, but she had a message for me.

"Tell Mary I love her more than she knows, and good-bye."

I could barely choke out, "Thank you so much for calling. Tell her I love her too and good-bye."

"She wants you to have the Buddhists in New York, the Taoists in Asheville, and everyone you know pray for her. She said you would know what she means," Bob said, a hint of laughter in his voice. Bob had once told me, "I don't know about this world you and Rhonda live in, but something about it works."

I promised I would make the calls and smiled, thinking of Rhonda's ability to continue to direct her care even in her final moments. As much as I wanted to be by Rhonda's side, I trusted that those who were meant to be with her were there. She had scripted her final scene just the way she wanted it to be.

Lama's First Call

Soon after Bob called the phone rang again. I had no desire to talk to anyone, but Brendan answered before I could say I wanted to be left alone. He handed me the phone.

"It's for you."

"Hello," I muttered, bereft.

An unfamiliar, soft, feminine voice said, "Hi Mary. This is Ani Jamdron calling from Kagyu Thubten Choling Monastery in New York. I'm sorry it's taken me so long to return your call. I understand you want to meet Lama Norlha when we come to North Carolina in a couple of weeks."

I was confused at first. Then I remembered that at Kathy's suggestion, I had tried to contact her Tibetan Buddhist teacher's teacher, Lama Norlha, to see if he would come to Chapel Hill when he was in Greensboro.

"Oh yeah, no problem…thanks for returning my call. I'm sorry, I'm out of it. I just found out my friend is dying."

She responded with sincere kindness.

"Jamdron is it?" I asked.

"Yes."

"My friend's name is Rhonda. A few weeks ago, and again tonight, she asked me to have you say *phowa* for her. Would you do that?"

"Yes, yes."

I was grateful for Jamdron's willingness to help someone she had never met. I made a couple of calls to alert others to pray for Rhonda. Then I went to my bedroom, lit candles and incense and fervently prayed. Even though I was confused about structured religion, sitting in prayer, like breathing, came naturally. I prayed for my best friend, for her family, for me. I prayed that she would not suffer. I prayed for comfort. I gave thanks for her life. I wondered what dying felt like; what she was going through.

Later that night, unable to sleep, I moved from room to room. At one point I wrapped myself in the soft mauve afghan that Rhonda had made for my new home. Curled in the fetal position on the couch, wrapped in the afghan, I sobbed deep, wracking sobs. I thought there were no more tears left in me. My stomach, my head, my whole body ached. How could it hurt so badly when we all knew it was coming? How in the world were Erin and Daniel surviving? Thinking of them and their loss, I cried even harder.

I got up and wandered into the guest bedroom, sat at the desk and began writing words that came from—I don't know where they came from.

Rhonda's Song

There's a whisper of you in my heart
There's a whisper of you in the sun
There's a whisper of you in all that I do
There's a whisper and it touches everyone

There's a song that you sing oh so clear
There's a song that you sing so profound
There's a song that you sing, the heavens they do ring
When I hear it, I feel you are near

There's a light and it shines with a blaze
There's a light and it shines for us all
There's a light and it shines to the heavens we are called
Like a whisper and a song and a light.

Dancing Naked Under the Moon

Part Two: Longing

"Compassion is not pity but a genuine 'being with' other persons, based on an awareness of interdependence."
—Matthew Fox

Love Thy Neighbor

We returned from the funeral tired, sad, and hungry. Van had taken over most of the parenting duties for the last few days. I was too disoriented to respond to the chatter and needs of eight-year-old Brendan and seven-year-old Kiki. As I walked through the door to our home in Chapel Hill, I felt a gnawing sense of hunger, but the thought of feeding the four of us overwhelmed me. How could making dinner seem so daunting? I had done it almost every day of my married life. Yet deciding what to eat, preparing the food, serving it—the daily tasks now seemed monumental. All I wanted to do was go to my room, curl up in bed, and let the exhaustion of grief wash over me.

The ringing doorbell jolted me out of my fog. When I opened the door, there stood my neighbor Nancy, homemade soup and bread in hand. Tears welled up in my eyes as I realized she was here to feed us. *To feed us.* In her take-charge way, Nancy placed the pot on the counter and enveloped me in a soft, loving embrace. When we stepped apart I saw care and concern in her luminous blue eyes. Her short, blonde hair framed her pale, round face. She looked much younger than her forty-something years—she seemed to me a modern-day Florence Nightingale.

In her Ohio twang, Nancy informed me that our neighbors were each preparing our dinner for the next week so that I wouldn't have to worry about cooking. I insisted that this was overkill, even though secretly I knew being fed and cared for was exactly what I needed. She met my protests with a forceful: "There's nothing to discuss. We've already arranged it."

I tried to say something, anything, but no words came—only a hard lump in my throat. I had lived on this street for a mere nine months, and it wasn't a family member I had lost. How had these women known I would need warm meals and soft shoulders? Over the next week, one neighbor after another visited. In her own way, each offered nourishment for our bodies and our souls. The generosity and compassion of my new friends filled me with comfort—and the desire to offer this same solace to others.

Wagon Magnolia

I was sitting on our white sofa looking out the bay window at the street. There was movement at the end of the cul-de-sac and I couldn't quite make out what was coming down the road. Slowly, the form took shape and I realized it was a group of children and adults walking together. Leading the pack was five-year-old Brad, a blonde-haired, blue-eyed "fireplug" with an infectious smile and a tender heart. He was pulling a red wagon with something tall in it. The procession ambled toward our house. When they turned into our driveway, I gasped. While Brad pulled the wagon, his father Gary stabilized its contents—a dwarf magnolia tree. I stepped outside.

"This is for you to plant in memory of Rhonda," my friend Terry, Brad's mom, informed me, shakily. Stunned, I attempted to dam the flow of emotions pressing against my chest with a feeble "Thank you."

Along with the magnolia tree, my neighbors planted a seed of hope in me—hope that if I could be so comforted and loved by community when I needed it most, others could be too. These neighbors weren't lifelong friends who had known Rhonda, but they were a community of individuals, bound by proximity, who chose to come together and give of themselves. These loving people responded in my time of need; we met on that common ground where all hearts have the opportunity to intersect—in those places of vulnerability and pain.

The Holy Spirit and Life Saver Necklaces

During the first months after Rhonda died, I moved as if there were a heavy, sticky film covering me. Making a pot of coffee took great effort. Frequently I realized Brendan or Kiki had been talking to me and I had drifted away from the conversation. My thoughts were cloudy; I didn't feel very sharp most of the time. The slightest interruption or intrusion made me irritable. Sometimes my turbulent emotions gyrated from sad to mad. I was pissed that my friend was gone, that Erin and Daniel had been robbed of growing up with their great mom.

I received an email from my sister Kathy alerting me to an upcoming visit by her Tibetan teacher, Lama Norlha. He would be speaking nearby. I wanted to meet the people who had stayed up and prayed for Rhonda on the night she died and to connect with the teacher who had such a profound impact on my sister. I ached for a teacher of my own. I drove over to the talk, numb.

Lama Norlha sat cross-legged at the front of the living room on a platform adorned with gold statues and bowls. Behind him there were Asian-looking banners in red and gold on the wall. Outfitted in traditional crimson and gold Tibetan robes, he appeared serious as he sat expressionless, nearly motionless. Lama Norlha's skin was cinnamon-toned; he had a shaved head, a round face and belly. Below and to the right of Lama sat a young American nun, also in crimson robes with a shaved head. She held a yellow notepad and a pen in her hands.

The ceremony began with a brief teaching from Lama. He spoke Tibetan in a low, gravelly voice, and in a staccato cadence unfamiliar to my American ears. The nun vigilantly wrote on her pad and then translated Lama's words to English. Sometimes she would stop writing, cock her head and rapidly ask a question of Lama in Tibetan. He would lean forward and speak directly, teacher to student, punctuating the important words with dramatic inflection. At some magical point, the nun would nod her head and reply, "so, so, so, so." Then she would turn to the group and share what she had learned.

"Happiness does not come from external things although they can be very alluring," the nun told us. "True happiness comes from being open-hearted, compassionate. When we feel ourselves pulled in a direction of despair, it is a good time to look for ways to support others."

What? These paradoxical words turned my saddened heart. Was there some way I could take my pain and redirect it toward helping others? I wondered. Even though I had been hard-pressed to take care of simple tasks for my family lately, the thought of reaching out to others who were hurting stirred me. The intensity of the moment felt like powerful experiences I used to have in church as a young girl. I wondered, "Does the Holy Spirit hang out in Buddhist ceremonies too?"

"It is important to understand that we find happiness in virtuous thoughts, speech, and actions," Lama said. This was the first of many times that I would hear those potent words.

After the teaching, we were instructed to chant in Tibetan and bow at the appointed times. I felt totally out of place and uncoordinated during most of the ceremony. I tried to act nonchalant, as if I belonged there, but I was a few seconds behind everyone when it was time to bow or prostrate. While we were bowing, I peeked up like a naughty child to make sure I was "doing it right." My chanting sounded more like my father's embarrassingly deep church singing than the melodious music ascending from the other participants. I was convinced everyone but me knew what they were doing. It was one of those horrible teenage-like moments when I wanted to fit in desperately. Yet, like an awkward teenager, the harder I tried to fit in, the more I stuck out.

At the end of the ceremony, the participants were encouraged to form a line to receive a necklace and a blessing from Lama. Hesitant, I waited and watched the others. I moved forward tentatively when it was my turn and bowed my head. Lama placed my face between his hands and touched my forehead to his. Heat penetrated at the spot where our heads met, a shiver jolted my spine. Muttering a blessing in Tibetan, he placed the necklace around my neck. It was a red string necklace with a white lifesaver-looking charm attached. (Later I learned that the charm was made from conch shell. The hole in the center is created by Tibetan nuns who put a section of the conch shells inside their prayer wheels. As the nuns pray, bamboo tubes in the wheels carve out the center of the shell. Each necklace was formed by countless turns of the prayer wheel and countless blessings.)

I started to walk out the door when I impulsively returned and approached the nun.

"I'm Kathy's sister, Mary. The one you helped by saying *powha* for my friend who died a few weeks ago."

"Mary, I'm Jamdron. I remember. How are you doing?" she asked.

"I'm okay, but it's hard, you know. Anyway, I wanted to offer for Lama to come and give a teaching in Chapel Hill if he would like. I would love to host him, all of you really."

"Thank you Mary. That is quite generous. I will be sure to tell Lama."

Swinging

Within days of our meeting, Ani Jamdron called to relay a message from Lama Norlha. He would accept my offer to visit and was coming to our home in a few weeks. Jamdron instructed me to let the Chapel Hill community know about his visit so those who were interested could attend an evening teaching.

"Could you find an appropriate venue for the teaching?" Jamdron asked.

I assured her that would not be a problem, hung up the phone and began a panicky serious of calls to pull together the event. I wanted everything to be perfect.

On the day of his visit, Lama arrived early and I was late, returning from a last-minute run gathering ingredients for a feast. Pulling into the driveway I groaned when I saw the white sedan with New York license plates parked in front of the house. Screeching my massive mommy-van to a halt, I threw open the door and ran around the outside of the house, trying to find my visitors. The house was locked and their car was empty. Where were they? I rushed to the backyard and stopped.

Round, smiling Lama Norlha was sitting on a wooden swing, gripping the metal links of the chain, his long, maroon robe flowing, legs straight, and feet pointing ahead. He was swinging on Brendan and Kiki's wooden swing set. I recognized his translator, Ani Jamdron, as the woman in robes gently pushing him from behind. When I approached Lama, his face opened into a carefree grin.

"I have never done this before," he said in a thick accent. "It is good!" Lama, Ani Jamdron, and Ani Palmo, another of the nuns, and I stayed out at the swing set for a while before heading inside for lunch.

Brendan and Kiki followed Lama everywhere. He matched their childlike demeanor and reveled in telling them about the pranks he pulled on the older monks as a young child living in the monastery in Tibet.

One morning Brendan and Kiki were mischievously peeking under Lama's bedroom door while he was chanting. He startled them by opening the door and inviting them to join him. Looking for the children so I could take them to school, I found them quietly sitting cross-legged in the circle with Lama and his apprentices. Brendan and Kiki were mesmerized by the chanting and ringing of cymbals.

"We're offering puffed rice and water and dedicating it to invisible beings that don't have enough to eat and drink," Jamdron explained at the conclusion of the ceremony. We stared blankly at her and she rephrased her explanation, "This is a symbolic offering of food and water for the needy."

Knowing they were late for school, Brendan and Kiki each

leaned over to Lama and let him take their faces in his hands, touching forehead to forehead in a tender good-bye.

Yuka's Kindness

This wasn't the first time I had been touched by the gentle spirit of a Buddhist. Five years earlier in Tokyo, there were nights when Kiki's asthmatic wheezing was bad enough that I had her sleep with me so I would know immediately if she needed a breathing treatment in the middle of the night. I would lie in bed with Kiki's soft toddler body draped across my chest, smelling her freshly-washed skin and hair, listening to her labored breathing. Drifting off to sleep, I would chant to myself the Japanese word for asthma, *zensoku*, and our address, *Meguro-ku, Ni-chome*, in case I needed to call an ambulance.

Our street resembled a mini-United Nations. Japanese, Americans, and Europeans coexisted in an environment of respect and community. Yuka, a young Japanese woman, lived across the street from us. She had attended college in Kansas and her understanding of the English language and American customs was indispensable to me. Yuka knew what it was like to feel lost in another country. I came to anticipate my morning ritual of sweeping soot off my front porch because often I would speak with Yuka at that time.

One morning, after a particularly grueling night with Kiki, I saw Yuka on her front porch holding her broom. Van had been out of the country; frequently his responsibilities at Nihon Sun required that he work late or travel overseas. Forcing a smile, I bowed slightly and greeted Yuka with a half-hearted, "*Ohayou gozaimasu*!"

"*Ohayou gozaimasu,* Mary-san, how are you today?" she responded cheerfully.

This time instead of hiding my fatigue and fear, I just sighed, "Worn out."

Yuka left her porch and approached me. I left mine and we

met in the middle of our narrow road, each of us leaning on our brooms.

She looked at me with great concern and asked, "What is the matter?"

"I'm exhausted from staying up all night with Kiki," I said. "I'm so afraid the emergency operator won't understand my English if we need an ambulance. If we do have to take her to the hospital, how will I communicate with them so they don't hurt her?"

Once I released the lock on the pressure-cooker of fear inside me, the overwhelming feelings began to bubble up and spill out of me. I added, "Besides, what should I do if there is an earthquake?" Yuka nodded her head with a grave look on her face. She didn't seem to think I was overreacting or crazy.

"Ah so…Mary-san, if you ever need to call an ambulance I want you to come and get me right away—anytime, day or night. Do not worry about waking me up. If Kiki needs to go to the hospital, I will go with you. It will be all right. You won't have to go alone." Yuka nodded her head confidently and added, "About the earthquakes, there is an emergency shelter at Komazawa Koen. If I am able, I will go with you. If not, simply take the children and there will be people to help you."

She smiled kindly, "It will be all right, Mary-san."

I looked into her soft, almond-shaped eyes and saw that she genuinely cared. She truly wanted to help. Yuka soothed my worried heart.

Like many Japanese, Yuka practiced both the Shinto and Buddhist religions. That might seem strange to Westerners, but it is totally natural in Japan. My relationship with Yuka offered an opportunity for me to reflect on the long-held precept that only Christians gained entry into heaven.

Driving home from taking the children to school and preparing to say good-bye to my guests, Lama Norlha and his entourage, I thought, how could Yuka, a Shinto/Buddhist woman full of Christlike kindness, be denied a seat at the table? Wasn't it arrogant for any one culture to claim they had the only path to God? Wouldn't God insist on the widest possible pearly gates? *Wouldn't God want to hang out with Yuka and Lama Norlha*? I began to wonder if the narrowing of the gates was the result of human interpretation or Divine inspiration.

Monday Meditations

When I returned home, I made tea for my guests before their long drive to New York.

"Mary, Ani Palmo will come here to teach meditation each Monday for the next four weeks," Lama proclaimed.

Palmo looked as surprised as I felt; I hoped she was as excited as I was.

For the next four Mondays, Palmo arrived at our home early in the day so we could have the entire afternoon to ourselves before the evening meditation class. One afternoon we took a blanket and picnicked in the woods behind the house. It was March; the time of year in North Carolina when the roadsides and woods are highlighted by the purples and pinks of the redbud trees. If weather was money this would have been a million-dollar day—clear, blue Carolina sky, the fresh smell of pine, filtered sun peeking through the trees.

Undaunted by her long, heavy robes, Palmo trekked over the rough terrain, keeping in step with me in my sneakers and jeans. We stopped at a hillside overlooking a creek. I unfolded the blanket, put the basket down, and sat across from Palmo. A few years my junior, she seemed like my younger, wiser, sister. With half a sandwich in my right hand and my left hand planted on the blanket, I turned to Palmo.

"I feel like I'm not doing much to contribute to the world," I said. "I mean, financially, I'm not helping our family at all. And look at you; you're traveling all over the southeast to help awaken people to living better lives. What am I doing?"

Silence hung in the air for a few moments.

"You're raising loving, conscious children," Palmo said. "Being a literal or figurative mother is one of the most important vocations. Whether you are the lover and caretaker of your blood or of a wider group, what is more important than that?

"So many times we focus on 'what' we are doing, rather than 'how' we are doing it. When I first went to the monastery, I was frustrated that we were cooking and cleaning rather than listening to teachings from Lama. At some point I finally realized that the cooking and the cleaning were an extension of my practice, if I did them mindfully."

We continued to chat easily during lunch, and then I reclined on the blanket, cradling my head in my hands. Although my stomach was full, my heart was hungry for understanding. I knew Palmo had intimate experience with grief. When she was twenty-one years old, her mother dropped dead of an aneurysm on a San Francisco street.

"Palmo, I miss Rhonda so much. When do you think the pain goes away?"

"Mary, it isn't that the pain ever goes away. Rhonda has given you great gifts. In her living she gave you the gifts of friendship and love." Palmo paused running her long fingers through the grass as if she was searching for words. Tilting her head she said, "In her dying she gave you the gift of true compassion for others. Losing Rhonda is intensifying your connection to all beings that have experienced sadness and loss. This is a window for you to have real empathy for all living creatures."

"This sounds like what I've been reading in Steven Levine's book," I said. "I love his story about the dying woman who connects her pain to *the* pain. Palmo, I'm trying to see my sadness in the context of connecting with the pain of others. When I do that, I feel like it gives meaning to my pain. But to tell you the truth, I usually just feel self-absorbed and sad. I'm not thinking about *the* pain, I'm thinking about *my* pain."

"It's as if you think you are supposed to be perfect," Palmo said, and smiled. "Maybe you could go easy on yourself."

"Yeah, that would be a new trick."

Again, silence.

"Okay, teacher, I have another question," I said, disturbing the quiet. "When we are doing the Chenrezig meditation practice for compassion, I have a hard time visualizing the Buddhist beings. It's not natural for me at all. I have a strong heart connection to Jesus and to Mary. Is it okay for me to visualize one of them instead of Chenrezig?"

"Yes, yes. What matters most is the love and the connection that you have with the enlightened being. Sometimes when I begin the meditation, I will instruct the students to visualize Chenrezig, or Mary or Jesus or Mohammed. As long as you see it as an enlightened guide or master, that is what matters."

Faith

I wanted to take the lessons Rhonda had taught me, lessons about how to live and how to die, out into the world. Thinking about end-of-life care became my obsession. Furiously I channeled my grief into laying the groundwork for starting a non-profit organization in her memory. I searched the Internet, learning about what other communities were doing to make people's dying experience better. My nightstand was piled with books such as Ira Byock's *Dying Well*, Elisabeth Kubler-Ross' *On Death and Dying*, and Stephen Levine's *A Year to Live*. A light began to shine on a whole new world for me, a world of care and support for people who were dealing with dying. I wished I had known about all these resources when Rhonda was sick. The more I read, the more I wanted everyone to know this information, and the more energized I became.

I came upon the Missoula Demonstration Project (MDP) in Missoula, Montana, a dynamic, community-based, end-of-life care non-profit. I called Barbara Spring, one of the founders of MDP, and she agreed to arrange a day for me to meet with her staff and have lunch with her. I was jazzed! My family was already planning to vacation in Montana. This would be perfect. I couldn't believe she would give me the time when I didn't even have an organization together yet. Besides, she was on sabbatical.

Missoula, Montana felt like a small-town version of granola-loving Berkeley, California. On my way to the meeting, I breathed Montana's humidity-free summer air and felt refueled. Missoula's manageable downtown had a charming John-Wayne-meets-Jerry-Garcia feeling. The Bitterroot Forest and three gorgeous rivers surrounded the town, adding to its appeal. The town made me feel a pang of longing for California; I knew I could live here.

Turning onto Main Street I found my destination. I was surprised that it was a mustard-colored home with dark green and burgundy trim and a wide and welcoming front porch. The wooden sign next to the front door read, "Missoula Demonstration Project: The Quality of Life's End." Somehow I had expected MDP to be located in an office building, not a house.

A young woman with long, brown hair greeted me from behind an antique desk and offered coffee. The rest of the morning was a whirlwind. I moved from room to room meeting with no fewer than ten staff members and volunteers. I instantly connected with these people, who shared my new passion and unselfishly offered their time and advice. Yellow legal pad on my lap, I wrote as fast as I could, flipping page after page, wishing I had brought a tape recorder so I could record their exact words. My head was spinning with new ideas. My heart, if it had a voice would have jumped out of my chest and screamed, "Thank you! Thank you!"

After finishing my morning with the staff and volunteers, I returned to the dining room-turned lobby and waited for Barbara. I had so much to ask her, I didn't know where to begin. A short, blue jean-clad woman in her middle fifties clomped down the stairs calling out a friendly, "Hey there, you must be Mary! We're heading to this fancy restaurant down the street—the Elk's Lodge. They have the best burgers in town."

Sitting across from Quaker-to-the-core Barbara, I was reminded of butterfly bushes—they thrive under any conditions. Barbara gave me the impression she was hardy, and could blossom anywhere. Over lunch, Barbara asked me, "Why do you want to start a nonprofit dealing with death and dying, anyway?"

I told her about Rhonda, and about losing Van's sister, Jill, to cancer. Tears, those damn tears that never seemed to stop, welled up in my eyes. Barbara's eyes moistened too. Overtaken by emotion, feeling safe with this near-stranger, I ranted about my indignation at the injustices families face when they lack the resources Rhonda had been blessed with—the top-notch medical facilities, financial stability, and emotional support. I told her after six years of being a stay-at-home mom, I was energized by this renewed sense of purpose; that it helped to create meaning out of losing Rhonda.

I didn't tell her everything. I didn't tell her that the more I worked, the less I cried; or that this frantic pace was a great diversion from the searing pain that radiated from my heart whenever I thought about how empty I felt in my marriage. Those were details I kept zipped in my "private thoughts" compartment.

After listening to my words, and perhaps sensing some of what was unsaid, Barbara asked if I wanted some suggestions.

"Of course, that's why I'm here."

"First, you're on the right track, kid. The world needs passionate people like you to create awareness." Barbara clapped her hands together for effect. "Let's face it. Everyone, everyone is impacted by death. It's just that no one wants to talk about it. By telling your story, you will give other people the courage to tell theirs. That's how we're gonna create change—by telling our stories. Yours is compelling. I'm so sorry."

She reached across the table and squeezed my hand.

"Thank you. It helps to be doing something. Do you know what I mean?"

"Oh, sure I do. I'm taking care of my mom, who lives me

with right now. I know. Let me ask you something. It sounds like you want to do something concrete for patients and families, not just community education. Is that true?"

"I think so. I don't know for sure. I have so many ideas and this is all so new to me."

"Well, I just went through this training in Birmingham, Alabama, with a guy named Malcolm Marler. Have you heard of him?"

"No, I haven't. What kind of training did you go through?"

"It's called Care Teams. It's an amazing way to organize volunteers. I think you might want to consider using his model for people who don't yet qualify for hospice. The average caregiver is giving care for more than four years. That's a long time if you don't have help."

I wrote on my pad, "avg. c.giver 4 yrs." I looked up at Barbara, willing her to continue. I couldn't soak the information up fast enough.

"If you can afford it, go to Birmingham and take their training. I think offering Care Teams would be a great way to get people in the community involved and create awareness that way."

Looking over at Barbara's soft, round face I felt exhilaration bubble up within me, and I saw it in her.

"Thanks for everything. I can't believe how much I've learned today. I'm impressed with what you've done here and frankly, I'm a little intimidated," I admitted.

Leaning forward I continued, "I've never done anything like this before, but I really, really want to make a difference. It's like if I don't, then Rhonda died for nothing." I surprised myself with the level of conviction in my voice.

"I think you've got what it takes, kid. I'll do anything I can to help you. By the way, what's the name of this organization going to be?"

I hesitated and decided Barbara was someone I could trust. She seemed to have faith in me, even though I didn't.

"Well, I'm not sure," I said, feeling hesitant. "But a few months ago when I was in the garden, the name Project Compassion kept going through my head. I'm actually chanting the Tibetan Buddhist practice Chenrezig right now—it's the practice for cultivating compassion. I just thought Project Compassion felt right. What do you think?"

"I love it. I love it. That's perfect. Project Compassion."

Hope

Before our trip to Montana, I had begun organizing a community event to promote an upcoming Bill Moyers' series on death and dying, called *On Our Own Terms*. When I returned to North Carolina, I focused on securing speakers for the event. Friends and people I had never met before stepped up in big ways to help pull together a fabulous panel of speakers for the program. The event was entitled, *Isn't It Time We Talk?* Most nights I would go to bed with only a fraction of my tasks crossed off of my to-do list. My days were never long enough to follow up on all the great leads for potential partners.

As the evening of the program approached, I felt anxiety. Would anyone come? Would the speakers be effective? Would my daily prayer be answered that those who were meant to hear the message would be present? I wanted the evening to be successful so that others would have the benefit of information I didn't have before Rhonda died. I also needed it to be successful so I would know that what I was doing mattered. I was on fire about this cause. If the turnout was light, what would that say about me and my mission?

Arriving at the Unity Center for Peace an hour before *Isn't It Time We Talk?* was scheduled to start, I scanned the rows of chairs to make sure they were all lined up. I placed a bottle of water on each of four chairs in the front row for the speakers. I felt the same adrenaline rush that I used to feel before important client meetings when I was a financial planner. I paced back and forth in the empty church.

The heavy wooden door opened and a medium-build man with curly gray and black hair strode toward me, smiling broadly. He placed a simple manila folder on one of the steel chairs and reached his hand toward me.

"You must be Mary. I'm Tony Galanos."

He gripped my hand with both of his. Tony and I had spoken on the phone at length. He was a geriatrician from Duke University and the medical director at The Forest at Duke, a local retirement community. He had strongly affirmed that the Chapel Hill area needed Project Compassion. The other speakers arrived—Jan Clark, a hospice chaplain, and several other medical professionals.

At the appointed time, I approached the podium. It had been a long time since I had spoken to a large group. Looking out at the audience, I felt my heart race. The small church was packed, there were over ninety people in the room.

"Based on the turnout tonight, I guess it is time we talked!" I joked. The audience chuckled; I was relieved.

The panel was impressive, informed, and engaging. Tony was the first to speak.

"I'm a little nervous being up here at the front of a church. I would be much more comfortable in a locker room!" Laughter again broke the hush in the room. From that moment on, the audience was riveted. Tony shared stories of his own and other families' anguish over making end-of-life decisions for their loved ones. He encouraged everyone in the room to communicate their health care wishes while they still could. Moving from the serious to the silly, Tony asked, "What is the most important factor that will ensure you'll get great care at the end of your life?"

Audience members called out answers such as money and health insurance.

Tony smiled and said, "No! Have daughters. Lots of daughters. I'm tellin' you, I see this all the time. It's the daughters who do the work!"

The hospice chaplain, Jan, went last.

"Mary has asked me to speak about spiritual care of the dying," she began. Then, grabbing the podium and looking skyward for effect, she continued, "Ever since hearing this request I keep wondering—how is that different from spiritual care of the living?"

In an emotional closing to the evening, Jan led us in a responsorial adaptation of "I Will Remember You" from Gates of Prayer. Gripping the sides of the lectern, leaning forward, Jan read the first line of each stanza in a booming voice. Those of us in the audience responded with a unified, resounding, "I will remember you" after each line. Our conviction and response grew louder with each stanza until Jan reached the final verse.

"As long as I live, and wherever I may go, you will be a part of me, because"

"I will remember you," we all responded.

Silence infused the room—ninety-plus hearts beating as one holy soul.

Contrary to what might be expected at the conclusion of a program on death and dying, the buzz was electrifying. After everyone left, I bolted shut the church door. Closing the door to Rhonda's hospital room had been impossible. Closing this door I felt a feeling I didn't even know I'd been missing—hope.

Love

Immediately, the pages in my Franklin Planner began to fill with notes and appointments. I was determined to find the right people to help volunteer and donate to this important cause. I felt driven, chased by the fear of failure. After years of focusing on my family's needs, I was consumed with having a purpose of my own. Late into the night, I would return to my computer to research one more funding source, or to fill out the necessary legal documents to become a non-profit.

People at Duke University, the University of North Carolina, and local faith communities rallied behind Project Compassion. Some played short-term roles. Others, like my neighbor and "sister of the soul" Elinor, made significant long-term commitments to the budding organization. From my first week in Chapel Hill, when she showed up with a chicken casserole, Elinor had nourished me—with food, counsel, and friendship. Her fair skin and brown eyes were framed by shoulder length, wildly curly hair, the color of fall, auburn. Trained as a therapist, she was a great listener with a quick wit and a big smile.

When I first began sharing my ideas about Project Compassion, Elinor would gently offer suggestions, ideas, and encouragement. She had a wealth of knowledge about grief, creative ideas about programs, and more connections than a New York switchboard. We walked our dogs in the woods and talked every day.

"Mary, I'm worried about how hard you are working," she often said. "My concern is that you're still grieving and you need to be careful not to burn yourself out."

There were many midwives who birthed Project Compassion. Elinor was the "mother of all midwives." While most of the people who became involved were caring, Elinor's presence provided me with something deeper that I sorely needed—love.

Shared Stories

The early days of Project Compassion were both a magical time of new connections and friends and a busy time of running from pain. Preferring the thrilling high of talking about my new passion, I chose to spend most of my time in that pursuit while avoiding the sadness I felt about losing Rhonda and living in a stress-filled marriage. Van and I seemed to be moving father and farther apart. I didn't yet know that the faster I ran away from that old linebacker, grief, the harder I would fall when it finally tackled me.

As more people came to know about Project Compassion's mission, momentum grew. Barbara Spring was right—everyone is touched by death and dying, and it is our stories that weave the connections. Repeatedly the right person would step in at the right time and bring his or her own special spark to the cause. Ultimately, they would have a personal or professional experience that compelled them to jump in and get involved. Each "yes, we need this organization" fueled my passion and encouraged me to keep moving forward. Each heartbreaking story fed my desire to create change; each heartwarming story inspired faith.

I made a lot of mistakes. Maneuvering around political landmines without a map meant that I occasionally stepped on one. Sometimes I was disillusioned by those few who could have helped but chose to sit idly by. Sometimes my overzealous and fiery personality got me into trouble. One time, frustrated and flabbergasted by the endless, fruitless meetings with a man who had access to millions of dollars for end-of-life programs, I blasted, "I'm concerned that your fear of making a mistake is greater than your ability to catch this vision!"

That approach didn't work very well. Because my mission was so closely tied to my grief, my perspective was skewed. I interpreted his negative responses as denials of Rhonda's importance, denials of my pain.

Care Team Training

I traveled to Birmingham to take Care Team training as Barbara Spring had suggested. I could not have known that on that trip I would meet two men who would become very important in my future.

The day before the training, Malcolm Marler met with me and another fledgling non-profit founder to answer our questions. The most memorable part of the meeting for me was my feeling of admiration for Malcolm, for the passion he brought to his work and his unconventional choice to leave church ministry to be a bridge between HIV/AIDS patients and faith communities. I was touched by the stories Malcolm told of how Care Teams had changed the care many of his patients received. I learned from Malcolm about the plight of HIV/AIDS patients and the stigma they experienced. He opened my eyes to a whole new world. After Malcolm patiently answered my endless questions, I was whisked away by a woman named Carol Padgett for a tour of the Balm of Gilead, a palliative care unit at the county hospital which was featured as an exemplary program in Bill Moyer's PBS special, *On Our Own Terms*.

Carol, the Community Education and CareSharing Coordinator, knew the patients and family members by name. In one room her question, "How's she doing today?" was met with the anguished face of a man about to lose his bride of more than fifty years. Small, olive-skinned, and wrinkled, the man spoke with a rural accent and shook his head sadly at Carol.

"Not so good today," he said. "They tol' me it may be close. It may be close."

Carol hugged him and they both cried. After a little while, the three of us were laughing and crying as he took us down his memory lane, sharing stories of his wife's antics.

That evening, Carol and her husband Ben invited me to join them for dinner, along with James Brooks, one of the training participants. At the time, James was a chaplain at a hospice in Tallahassee, Florida. He was attending the training because he had been using the Care Team model to organize hospice volunteers.

James and I spoke the same language immediately. As we ate fried catfish and swapped tales, I listened in awe as James described the programs he had started in Tallahassee. I laughed at his funny stories about organizing volunteers. Although he was in his late thirties, James looked much younger. His boyish, round face belied the fact that he was an intense man, driven to succeed and passionate about improving the dying experience. The next day James and I sat together at the training Malcolm led. I was grateful for James' advice and friendship. Little did I know that I was talking with Project Compassion's next executive director and learning about Care Teams from my future husband.

Unfurling

A plan began to emerge to create Project Compassion as the hub of a wheel, providing the community with information and support. I felt ill-prepared to be at the helm of this entity, yet I couldn't imagine handing it over to anyone else. Some nights after putting the kids to bed, I would collapse into a chair, glass of wine in hand, and wonder, "Why the hell am I doing this?" Inevitably within a couple of days some new exciting development would transpire and I'd be pumped up to march on.

Compelled by grief, needing to create meaning out of Rhonda's death and wanting to keep her memory alive, I continued to tell my story. Patient, loving people listened and responded. In the beginning I naively behaved as if I were the first person to experience the loss of a deep love. I began to understand that although my experience was unique, there were many who also had experienced great loss. With each telling, my heart would heal just a little more. With each listening, it would break open again. As the tide's coming in and going out washes over the sand, this flow of telling and listening, listening and telling, washed over my heart. Stories helped to mold the organization's mission—a mission of presence and witness, a mission of support.

Overall, Brendan and Kiki adjusted to my busier schedule relatively well. Usually they took my constant telephone conversations and the declining quality of our mealtime offerings in stride. They also took an interest in my new passion. Kiki loved the day we spent with colored pencils and sketch pads trying to create a logo. Brendan would usually ask, "How'd ya do?" when I returned from an important meeting. Like all normal kids, they sometimes resented my project's intrusion into their lives, and once in a while my "in a minute" was met with eye-rolling, foot-stomping protest.

When he could, Van did his best to fill the parenting and household gaps. Both of us underestimated the strain my returning to work as a full-time volunteer would cause our already-troubled marriage. In fact, my job was costing both time and money. Like the goddess of justice, Themis, I held a scale. My new passion, Project Compassion, was on one side, and my dying marriage on the other. One or the other often needed more than I had to give, and I rarely felt a state of balance. My heart was alive with this new venture; I feared I would have to choose between it and Van.

Circle

Eleven months after Rhonda died and four months after *Isn't It Time We Talk?* the first Project Compassion Advisory Committee meeting was held. We met at the tranquil home of my friend, Lynne, an artist who lived with her husband in a spectacular, rustic, contemporary home overlooking a meadow, woods, and a picturesque pond. Tall, thin and almost girlish, Lynne's natural beauty imbued everything she touched. Hand her a bouquet of flowers, and she would arrange them effortlessly in just the right vase

On January 13, 2001, sixteen passionate, committed people representing the medical, therapeutic, and spiritual communities came together. Each of us was driven by our own experiences of grief and loss and hope; driven to make dying a normal part of living. We convened in a circle in Lynne's spacious living room. Surrounded by glass, it felt as though we were sitting in Lynne's garden and not inside a home. Wooden statues of horses, Native American art, feathers, and candles provided ambience—reminding us that we were in a special, spiritual space. Meredith, a consultant with years of non-profit experience, facilitated the group and kept us focused.

"What will be different five years from now if Project

Compassion succeeds?" Meredith asked.

"Nurses will feel appreciated and won't be burned out."

"Patients will enter hospice care sooner and stay longer."

"People won't be afraid to talk about dying."

"No one will die alone."

"Death won't be considered a failure."

Ideas flowed. We developed the beginning of a plan. A small group of us volunteered to meet regularly with Meredith to complete the plan.

At the end of the day, Meredith went around the room and asked each of us to offer a word that represented how we felt. Words like, "hopeful," "encouraged," "inspired," "motivated," and "excited" filled the room. When I was given the opportunity to express my gratitude, words seemed inadequate. Looking around the circle, I connected with each new friend. I was grateful for the grace that had brought all of us together. Here it was at last, the organization, the purpose I had been searching for.

Dancing Naked Under the Moon

Part Three: Leaving

"…determined to save the only life you could save."
—Mary Oliver

Breaking Vows

On May 25, 1985, in front of family and friends, I had vowed to spend the rest of my life in marriage to Van—through any joyous and difficult times we would endure. By 2001, I was no longer living those vows. Somehow over the course of our sixteen-year marriage, I had allowed myself to leave the relationship, spiritually and emotionally. I no longer accepted Van for who he was and I wasn't supportive of what he wanted to become. We weren't working as partners; we were competing like spoiled children—competing for time, competing for money, and weirdest of all, competing for "spiritual superiority."

It hadn't always been this way. Early on we were very much in love and working toward common goals. We would dream about becoming parents, reaching our professional benchmarks, and visiting interesting places. Like all long-term relationships, ours had its problems. And for many years we seemed to find a way, despite our diverging views, to come back together again.

There was one mistake, however, that I made over and over again: pushing aside and not communicating my true feelings and needs. I'm sure there were many factors that contributed to the end of our relationship, but this was perhaps the most detrimental. Whether I withheld my heartfelt desires because I thought I didn't deserve them or in order to keep the peace, the end result was the same. By submerging my true feelings, I allowed cracks to form in the foundation of our relationship.

Because some of my own needs were left wanting, I undermined the gifts I had given Van; I attached invisible strings. The setup was deadly from the start. When I chose to support Van in getting his MBA, I expected, yet never communicated, that one day he would support my getting a masters degree too.

East-West School

Soon after we returned from Tokyo and moved back to Northern California, I did enroll in a masters of transpersonal psychology program at JFK University. Living in Tokyo had opened me to new thoughts and ideas. I was fascinated by the intersections between East-West philosophy, psychology, and religion. The JFK curriculum was ideal.

One of my first classes was world religions with Dr. Vernice Solimar. Only a little over five feet tall, with dark skin and curly hair, Dr. Solimar was a force—a benevolent force, but a force nonetheless. I listened devoutly as she told magnificent stories. Raised in Spanish Harlem, she spoke of her Latino heritage, her study of the Christian mystics, and her choice to enter and then leave the Sisters of Charity religious community. Like me, she was spawned in a Catholic stream yet chose to swim in a wider river; one which includes the beauty of the Christian faith as well as the transformative aspects of other traditions.

I marveled at the depth of her firsthand experiences with people of different religions. When she told tales of carpooling with Orthodox Jewish men to New York City, we learned about the challenges these men faced living in a modern world. Speaking of her summers in the Amazon, she introduced us to the spirits that travel with indigenous tribes in South America. When Dr. Solimar recalled working beside a Muslim man, we learned about the popularity of Islam among some African American women.

I was engrossed. Each Thursday night before the babysitter arrived, I would throw a simple dinner on the table for Brendan and Kiki. As soon as the sitter walked in the door, I would quickly kiss the children and dash out the door to class. I was intoxicated with the intellectual stimulation of our class discussions, eager to be part of a community after my solitary studying. A seed that had been planted in me long ago took root in that class. Each week this love of learning about different traditions was nourished by the reading and discussion. Something in me blossomed.

We read Huston Smith's *The World's Religions*, Ann Bancroft's *Weavers of Wisdom*, and many other enlightening books. One spring day I drove to my favorite spot at the top of Mt. Diablo to read my homework. The mountain was quiet. It was the middle of the day in the middle of the week, and hardly anyone else was around. I parked my gold Honda Accord, grabbed the *Tao Te Ching* and hiked to a secluded spot. Sitting under the canopy of a California oak tree, I absorbed the expansive beauty of the Diablo Valley. Soaking in the natural wonders surrounding me, I felt my breathing slow down. My eyes scanned the horizon and I watched the hawks circle. When they called out to one another, they called to something deep within me.

I decided to lie back on roots and dirt and hold the book up to read.

The Master observes the world
but trusts his inner vision.
He allows things to come and go.
His heart is open to the sky.

Overpowering sleepiness swept over me, but I read a little more.

Do you have the patience to wait
till your mud settles and the water is clear?
Can you remain unmoving
till the right action arises by itself?

I set the open book across my chest, closed my eyes and entered a mystical state that is difficult to describe. What I remember most is the feeling that my body dissolved into the mountain and there was no boundary between me and the dirt—like snow melting into the earth. My breath was linked to the breath of the mountain. I felt peace-filled and blissful. I have no idea how long I lay on the ground that afternoon. When I finally sat up, I squinted into the blinding sunlight and tried to re-orient myself. Although unable to understand the experience, I knew that something in me was forever changed.

Feeding the Monster

At the same time this new world was opening for me at JFK, Van was feeling unfulfilled and frustrated with his career. The pressures of his job were significantly greater than the joy he felt in doing it. I was worried about him and wanted him to be happy. Even though I was devastated by the thought of discontinuing the program I loved at JFK University, I offered to defer my degree so that Van could pursue his dream of yoga teacher training. I felt guilty that I wasn't making money and we were paying for me to go to school. It seemed that my dream cost him too much, so I put mine on hold. Ever the martyr, I offered this gift with one hand while feeding the monster of resentment with the other.

Over and over again during the course of our marriage, I sabotaged what I wanted and needed by placing others' needs first. I brewed a toxic concoction of animosity in myself. Susan St. James, explaining why she and her husband chose not to sue the airplane company responsible for a plane crash that killed her son, revealed the insight of a woman who knows how to live, knows how to forgive. St. James said, "Resentment is like taking poison and then waiting for the other person to die."

I drank the poison over and over again, each time allowing pieces of myself and my marriage to die. Like logs on a flame, my repressed anger fueled my internal fury. When the fire erupted to the surface, sixteen years' worth of fuel blazed into a wildfire—creating devastation and destruction.

When our marriage was in peril, we didn't approach our difficulties as a team. We each focused on what we wanted individually. Ironically, Van's complaints mirrored my own—a sense of lost dreams and honor denied. Instead of freely giving of myself, I became more and more focused on what I felt he should or shouldn't be doing. The late psychotherapist Virginia Satir talked about the importance of "taking out the trash" every day in our relationships. I was accumulating a mountain of debris and becoming adept at walking around the pile, denying the growing stench.

Rhonda's death had challenged me to evaluate all of my relationships. Losing Rhonda forced me to look at my relationship with God, with Van, and with myself. It became clear to me that I could no longer waste my life. After watching Rhonda lose hers, I now deemed my own precious life as too valuable to waste in a relationship that was stagnant and unhappy. I could no longer continue to hide behind the needs of others in order to play it safe and deny my own needs. Rhonda had given me the deep trust and intimacy many of us hope for in our marriages. When I lost her unconditional support and presence in my life, the loneliness in my marriage began to overwhelm me.

Before choosing to end my marriage, I tried to find constructive ways to communicate what I wanted and needed, but I had drifted so far from myself that I didn't even know what I wanted. How could anyone else possibly know, when I didn't? All I knew was that I felt a strong desire to pursue my dreams, my goals, and my life purpose. Yet every step I took toward wholeness seemed to be a step away from Van.

Like patients who believe that ignoring symptoms and staying away from the doctor will quash illness, Van and I waited until our marriage needed life support before going to counseling. Treatments that might have been effective earlier were no longer viable.

The year prior to Van's moving out was filled with many difficult, frustrating, and gut-wrenching discussions. Family vacations were clouded with disagreements about time and money, over and over again, time and money. Who was going to get to "do" what; who was going to "pay" for what.

We ripped through two therapists in short order, showing

up at the first one's office when the tension in the house had become nearly unbearable and we frequently ended the day in separate bedrooms. With this therapist I felt defensive, like both the therapist and Van thought I should "get with the program" and go back to being a "good wife." An argument between Van and me ensued.

We had reached a point where these discussions never created any understanding, only more pain. We might as well have been standing at opposite sides of the room screaming at the walls. Neither one of us was listening to the other because we were both too busy trying to be heard. The therapist's small, cozy office felt like a coffin. I wanted to scratch my way out so I could breathe.

Driving home together I stared out the window, my anger evolving into immobilizing sadness. What was I doing? Was Project Compassion really worth this? I loved Van. He didn't beat me. He didn't drink. He didn't fool around. He was a good provider. Couldn't I just back off? Wasn't my family worth more than this crusade?

When we pulled into the driveway I looked over at the man who had been a huge force in my life for nearly twenty years. He looked drawn. Thin by nature, he was emaciated. I wanted to hold him. This was killing both of us. What was it doing to our kids?

"I'll consider quitting this whole Project Compassion thing and getting a job for pay. I don't even know what I would do right now, but I'm just saying I'll think about it."

"That would be good. I don't want to have to work so much. I want both of us to share more in the financial responsibility and then I'll help more around the house and with the kids."

Emotionally drained, I felt a fresh batch of sadness cook up in me as I thought about leaving my treasured new life. Thinking of all the skills I had developed and the people I had organized, I looked over at Van.

"Well, I'm proud of how far I've come with this. At least I know I've learned a lot by starting Project Compassion."

"Do you really think so?" he asked. I stared at him in disbelief. There was no sign of malice on his face. He had no idea the impact of his words. I turned my head, pain shooting down my back, and stared blankly out the window. "I've been here before," kept drumming in my head. "I've been here before." I'd been here when I decided to stay home full-time, when I agreed to move to Tokyo, and when I left JFK. How many times had I felt as if Van would go, "I'm giving you this gift" and then—swish, "I'm taking it away"? We both were committing the same crime—feeding resentment's insatiable appetite. Staring out at the wall of trees in our backyard I knew, "I cannot leave another dream for him or I will die." I kept my decision private. Even though I loved him, he was no longer a man I could trust.

Being the Monster

I felt selfish for putting my needs ahead of what I thought was probably best for Brendan and Kiki. Confusion ruled my life. How could having parents in separate homes be good for the children? How could living with parents who are unhappy be good for them?

Why couldn't I just make myself happy? This was the hardest question of all. I had everything I thought I wanted—a beautiful home, healthy, loving children attending a great school, and a supportive community. Yet the emptiness inside was like an abyss that was getting deeper and deeper with each passing day. What was missing? Why couldn't I just be happy? Why was I willing to risk so much when everything should have been fine?

Even though I couldn't answer these questions, I felt a compelling clarity every time I considered living apart from Van. I needed to hear my own voice again and I had been allowing his to drown out mine. Never having lived alone, I wanted to experience making my own choices, at least for a little while. I hoped that if we moved apart we could eventually reconnect, with a fresh marriage. I knew that if we chose to continue on the path we were heading, I would die. Whether it meant coming back together with Van in a new way or starting over on my own, I was convinced my life depended on being on my own, at least for a short spell. I was drowning in unhappiness and unfulfilled dreams and I needed to throw myself a lifeline. It was time for me to turn some loving energy inward and heal the woman who was crying out inside of me. Those flight attendants knew what they were talking about when they would instruct passengers, "If you are traveling with small children, put your own oxygen mask on first, then the child's mask."

I hoped if I could start breathing good air again I would be a better mom, a better person.

Telling Brendan and Kiki that their parents were separating was one of the hardest conversations of my life. We sat ten-year-old Brendan and nine-year-old Kiki down in the family room and explained that we had something important to talk to them about. We tried to assure them that we hoped this move was temporary, that Daddy would be nearby, that we loved them both so much, that our living apart had nothing to do with anything they had done, blah, blah, blah. All the books I had read on divorce and all the dress rehearsals I had performed in my head did not prepare me for the shocked look of fear on Brendan's face. His big brown eyes were unblinking in disbelief. Kiki's reaction was almost worse—helpless resignation.

As a mother, I had always tried to make choices that were in Brendan and Kiki's best interests. Looking into the shell-shocked eyes of my children, I wasn't sure I was on solid footing with this decision. As a woman I was pulled toward a sense of freedom I hadn't felt for years, maybe ever. As a mom I was afraid I was causing my children deep harm. How could I willfully inflict pain on my own children? I felt like a monster.

After our talk, I took Brendan and Kiki to Amelia Island to visit my parents. Gripping the steering wheel, cruising down I-95, I fielded question after question after question. Most of the inquiries came from Brendan. "Why didn't you and Daddy want to stay in the same house?" "When will I see Daddy?" "Will we still have holidays together?" "Who will take me to school?" "Where will I sleep at Daddy's new apartment?" "Where will my clothes go?" "Will Boomer and Daisy go to Daddy's with us?"

At one point, Brendan looked at me with a tearful grimace and said, "But you and Daddy were so good together."

Most of Brendan's questions gave me a chance to try and calm his fears and to feel like a loving mom again. The hardest part was answering, "I don't know" to the biggest question of all, "When will Daddy move back home again?"

He never did.

Slow Burn

Kiki and I danced across the hardwood floor in our two-person New Year's Eve celebration. We snapped our fingers and kicked up our heels to the *Princess Diaries* CD she loved. "Little bitty pretty one, I been watching you grooooowww…." Twirling away from each other and then coming close together again, we moved to the beat. "ohhh-ohhhhhh bop bop da bop…."

We danced in a frenzy until the end of the song, when we collapsed in a heap of arms and legs and laughter. Moments before, Van had left for his first night in his apartment, an apprehensive Brendan in tow. Our dance was less "dancing on the grave," and more a releasing of pressure. We were relieved of the tension that had enveloped the house for the past year.

For the first few months on my own, I continued to feel exhilarated, relieved, and free. Reconnecting with what I wanted, feeling a sense of control over my life I hadn't felt in a long time, I enjoyed my new independence. One kid-free night, I invited three girlfriends over and we drank wine and whooped it up watching *Sex in the City*. Another time I pulled out my acrylic paints and a blank canvas. With Beethoven playing in the background, I lost myself in each stroke of the brush.

Having convinced myself that most of my troubles were really Van's and not mine, I fostered the illusion that all was well. But over time, reality crept in and I was forced to address both my part in, and the difficulties around, ending my marriage. My attempts to push reality away by occupying my time with Project Compassion meetings, Brendan and Kiki's activities, and a frantic social calendar were unsuccessful. Even though Van was out of the house, my unsettled state returned.

At first, having every other weekend off from parenting responsibilities felt liberating. I visited Duke Gardens and other magnificent places, spending as much time as I wanted. I relaxed in yoga classes, read without interruption, and rented movies that only I wanted to watch. Listening to my wants and desires and responding to them filled me with a newfound satisfaction. Yes, in the beginning it was great to be able to call a girlfriend and go out without having to negotiate the "time off."

Over time all that changed. I questioned my decision to walk away from the familiar and into the unknown. In the words of Pema Chodron, the Buddhist writer, "It was one of those crises where everything fell apart. I couldn't feel any ground under my feet. It was devastating."

Like the primitive woman's long trek into the woods, my walk away from my former life became more difficult as time passed. Loneliness and anger crept in. Darkness too. Most of my girlfriends had families to be with when I wanted company. In the past, I would unselfconsciously go to parties alone when Van traveled; now I was painfully aware of my singleness. As the novelty wore off, a lifetime of unaddressed anger erupted and I found myself picking ridiculous fights with Van.

When I confided my insane behavior to Karen, my recently-divorced childhood friend, she responded in her thick New Jersey accent.

"Give yourself a break, Mare. The way I look at it, the first six months after splitting up you have an excuse for being crazy. If it goes on longer, get help." I reminded myself of Karen's advice countless times and I did get help.

Although I pretended to manage my new life quite well, dark thoughts occupied more of my time and brain than I care to admit. One particularly magical spring day, Kiki was home sick and wanted me to play with her. When I look back, I realize how often Brendan and Kiki stayed home with various ailments during that first year of the separation. It was as if their bodies could not hide the truth, even as they tried to be upbeat. Their little worlds were falling apart, their hearts cracking.

I was sitting at the kitchen table poring over bills when Kiki approached me, her big, brown eyes sparkling. She grinned, innocently. Holding a board game in her outstretched hands, she asked, "Mommy, will you play with me?"

"No, Kiki," I snapped. "Can't you see I'm busy?"

Sure I was busy; I was busy with my anger. Watching my little girl walk away, sad and dejected, and knowing I was the one who had extinguished the sparkle in her eyes, I decided the time had come to get this resentment in check. Not only was my rage poisoning me, it was also contaminating my children. Somewhere in the course of leaving my marriage, I had allowed "hardening of the heart."

Unfortunately, this "hardening of the heart" was seeping into all of my relationships—my relationship with God, with myself, my family, my friends, and the people at Project Compassion. Simmering beneath my extroverted smile and caring nature lived a slow burn, never far from the surface. I remember my dear friend Mindy saying, "I wouldn't want to mess with you when you are mad."

What is she talking about? I thought. I am nice and kind and compassionate!

But Mindy was picking up on the fire within, which I was trying to smother.

Walking away from the life I had spent thirty-eight years

creating scared me. I identified so strongly with my role as "Van's wife," I didn't know who I was as a single woman. I found myself responding with irritation at almost every turn. During meetings for Project Compassion, I felt frustrated and wondered why people took so long to "get it." I would snap at those who were trying to help. I spewed my enmity on the phone to my sisters. I composed countless unsent emails to Van. I wrote line after line, day after day, in my journals about how I had been unappreciated, misunderstood, and taken for granted.

In one particularly caustic journal entry, which represented my "take no personal responsibility" philosophy at the time, I wrote, "I haven't been emotionally supported in much of this marriage. I am blown away that Van thinks that his 'spiritual path' requires a significant amount of time away from his family. Seems like spiritual masturbation to me. I keep thinking he'll get it. We could be your spiritual path—right here, me, Brendan, Kiki…it's a fucking path!" What I couldn't acknowledge at the time was that my path required being away from family at times too.

Truth Telling

Before asking for the separation, I had spent countless hours in prayer and therapy, contemplating the best path for all who would be affected. When I finally made the decision to leave my marriage, I felt so Spirit-led. What had happened to my generous spirit? Why was this path so *hard*?

When I was deciding if Van and I should divorce or reconcile, I replaced the Tibetan chanting I had been doing for nearly a year with praying the rosary. Every day I would pull out the pink rosary beads that Rhonda and I had shared, chanting the prayers in a pocket-sized novena from my mother. A novena includes twenty-seven days of praying for a specific petition followed by twenty-seven days of giving thanks for the granting of the petition, (whether it has been granted yet or not). During this unstable time, my daily petition was, "to be more loving and open-hearted."

The unexpected answer to my prayer came one morning when I was driving past the woods, the area that I had called my "church," where I had enjoyed so many sacred moments. While I was driving, a calm, feminine voice rose up from within and said in an assuring tone, "The most loving thing you can do is end this marriage."

What? How could ending a marriage be loving? Where was this voice coming from? Who was speaking? Yet I knew in all of my being that "The most loving thing you could do is end this marriage" was the voice of wisdom—and truth.

On my journey away from the old I knew, I had to be completely honest with myself. Truth isn't always pretty. In fact, lots of times it's hideous, but perpetuating any lies would mean a journey back to my old life. Being honest was scary, but the thought of going back was paralyzing. My truth-telling journey started by being straight with Van about not wanting to reconcile, and it continued with admitting that my anger was destroying me and the people I loved. I wanted to face this pain, understand it, and create a new way of being. I didn't want to push it under the rug and pretend it wasn't there. I didn't want it to run my life anymore.

I had to face the difficult fact that all was not well with Brendan and Kiki. As I mentioned, their health suffered greatly during the first year after Van and I separated. Frequently I would get home from the hour round-trip drive to their school, and the phone would ring.

"Could you come and pick Kiki up? She isn't feeling well." Or, "Brendan's coughing is disturbing the class; could you please come and take him home?"

Sometimes I wanted to say, "No! I just got here and I have so much to do, and I'm so tired…can't you just take care of them?" Isn't that terrible of me, their mother? Yes, it's terrible, but it's true.

Of course their emotional health suffered too. Parent-teacher conferences were hell that year. Before, I had loved parent-teacher conferences. I loved hearing about all my children were doing. I preened proudly when I heard how diligently they worked, how successful they were. However, this is not what happened at Brendan's fifth-grade and Kiki's fourth-grade conferences.

That was the year parent-teacher conferences required Van and me be in close proximity, as separated mommy and daddy, publicly for the first time. It was awkward. This annual ritual, which we had in past years attended together with enthusiasm, was now another reminder of what was no more. When we met in the parking lot, I wondered, *Should we hug*? And *Which parent should take charge of the meeting*?

All the rules had changed. We went into Kiki's classroom first and met with Pam and Jeff, her teachers. There we were, four adults scrunched into child -sized chairs going over the detailed evaluation, when kind-hearted, first-year teacher Jeff couldn't hold back anymore.

"Kiki is so withdrawn, I'm worried about her. At the beginning of the year she would come in, put her backpack in her cubby and start playing with the other kids. Now she just grabs a book and sits alone. We've been trying to draw her out, but she resists. I just don't know what to do to help her."

Stunned and ashamed, we didn't know what to say. Next, we shuffled over to the fifth grade room for Brendan's conference—more of the same.

When we had first separated, Van and I were not clear with each other, the kids, and our carpool partners about where the kids would be each day. Inexperienced with this new way of parenting, we devised a confusing and disruptive schedule based upon a misguided perception that maximum flexibility would be best for the kids. One effect of the disjointed schedule was a falling-out with our carpool partners. Like nearly every other relationship in my life, even this peripheral friendship was changing. Everything was changing.

Having lived in Tokyo and California, I have experienced a number of earthquakes. Feeling the earth roll and shift, watching furniture move and pictures fall off the walls evokes a terrifying feeling of groundlessness. My life had become one earthquake after another. I didn't know what to hold on to for safety and I feared the next aftershock.

***

The post-separation financial tremors took me by surprise. For the past sixteen years I had found much of my identity in being married to a relatively successful dot-com executive. I had placed so much value on net worth, on things—what I owned, my investments, my home, my car. Since these things were dwindling fast, I had to look at who I was without them. Between accumulating stock in the company Van worked for and investing in the California real estate market, we had established a decent cushion for the future. I had come to believe the illusion that this cushion would continue to grow. I used to track its progress daily. I never imagined that in just six months, because of the dot-com collapse and expenses incurred by dividing households, not only would the entire cushion be wiped out, but I would accumulate a mountain of debt.

I had spent years working as a financial consultant, but at this time I broke every prudent planning rule I knew. It is a testimony to the dysfunction and pain we were experiencing at the time, that Van, who had a master's degree in finance, and I, with an undergraduate degree in finance and a Chartered Financial Consultant designation, did nothing when our Sun Microsystems investment dropped in value from over $700,000 to $24,000. Paralyzed by fear and unable to communicate effectively with Van, I watched the dot-com bubble burst without protecting my investments. We pretended that the fires of financial hell were not burning all around us. At the time, we couldn't effectively communicate about simple carpool schedules. There was no way we could tackle the incendiary big stuff, like money.

Afraid that no one else could do the job, I continued to work too long for little or no pay at Project Compassion. Unable to imagine moving from the home and the neighborhood that the kids and I loved, I held on too long to the big mortgage and dug a hole of debt that would be difficult to climb out of. With Donald Rumsfeld-like denial, I refused to honestly face the impending crisis until it was impossible to ignore.

Losing nearly every financial asset that I had owned required letting go of one of the greatest lies of all—the lie that there is such a thing as financial security. My losses forced me to realize that I had been worshipping at the empty altar of the "money gods." I had placed my faith and trust in the prestige, power, and freedom that comes from being one of the "haves." Things had come to own me rather than me owning them. By holding on to the image I had so carefully created, I closed off reasonable options, like selling my home or scaling back my lifestyle—actions that would have buffered the financial blow of divorce. Intellectually I knew better; emotionally I couldn't imagine living differently. What would people think?

When I finally started to honestly address the financial beliefs that were burying me, I wanted to renounce them and take responsibility for the "knight in shining armor" fairy tale that I fostered. During our marriage, rather than placing my trust in my ability to support myself, I had placed it in Van. By choosing not to produce an income, I had not taken responsibility for my financial needs. In fact, I was happy to hand them over to Van.

I am forever grateful for those long-gone days I had enjoyed as a stay-at-home mom with Brendan and Kiki. However, by investing only in Van's career, I had neglected to invest in me. When I finally hit the pavement, divorced and looking for a job, I found that my experience was out-of-date and I was only qualified for entry level or commission-based sales.

As time went on and one door after another closed, my

confidence eroded. Since leaving the workforce I had told myself, "I am worth a lot of money in the marketplace. I can reenter whenever I am ready," and "Choosing to stay home with my kids won't hurt me financially." After eight unsuccessful months of looking for a job I realized that my path to financial independence was steep indeed.

My thoughts and prayers changed from being confident, clear, and positive to desperate pleas for help. I knew I wanted to squelch the rage that consumed me and find a sense of peace again. I knew I wanted to find solid footing somewhere; I just didn't know where to begin.

You Should Go Home

Prayer had always steadied me in life's storms. But when my confusion centered on how to pray, and who to pray to, I became befuddled. Lama Norlha and Ani Palmo had changed my life, but calling Buddhism "home" felt unnatural. Weekday mornings would start with chanting in Tibetan and Sundays I would bounce around from one Christian church to another. None of them felt like home, either. Even though the Christian services had a sense of familiarity, I was alienated by any focus on rules and salvation, as opposed to following the example of Jesus' life. Most troubling was the treatment of women and homosexuals in the name of Christ. The teachings of some churches were antithetical to my sense that God's love flowed for all people, not just those who said the right things or lived the right life. On the other end of the spectrum, I was turned off by one church where I felt the message of personal abundance superseded the message of social justice. I longed for community, but didn't know where I fit in. I couldn't tell if I was being too critical of my options or true to my beliefs.

Looking for guidance, I traveled to Charlottesville, Virginia, to Lama Norlha's retreat center. During the weekend, Lama was available to meet privately with any of the students.

At my allotted time, I climbed the stairs and waited in one

of the two straight-backed chairs in the hallway outside of Lama's room. There was a small coffee table between the two chairs. Lama Norlha opened the door and stepped into the hallway. Standing up, I placed my palms together in front of my heart, bowing to Lama. Gathering his robes and sash, he sat down, and then I did.

"Lama Norlha, I don't know how to say what I want to say." I fidgeted with the end of my shirttail.

He looked at me, expressionless, silently waiting.

"I'm so grateful to you and Ani Palmo, and Ani Jamdron. You have changed my life. I'm just having a hard time saying, 'I'm a Buddhist.' And even though many times when I chant, I feel a Divine Presence, I find it confusing working with the Tibetan tradition and scrambling it in my American brain. Even though the teachings on mindfulness, loving kindness, and compassion have been so helpful…Lama, I'm sorry." I stammered, "I don't know what I'm doing wrong. Something is missing."

I felt so ashamed that I couldn't just "follow the program."

Lama sat quietly for a few minutes, and then he stood up. I rose and turned toward him. He took my face in his hands and gazed at me with his penetrating, dark, round eyes.

"You were raised a Christian. Perhaps it is time you should go home," he said, adding, "but it is very important that whatever path you choose, go deeply. Go deeply." Touching our foreheads together, he turned around and reentered his room, leaving me alone in the hallway.

Go deeply into what? I thought. Go deeply where?

I wanted Lama to choose for me. I wanted him to tell me what I could do to be a better Buddhist. I thought maybe if I just heard the right words from him I would fit in. He didn't do that, though. He lovingly gave my struggle back to me and challenged me not only to make a choice, but to commit all of who I was to that choice. I had never done that before. I had always kept one foot in and one foot out. It felt safer that way. Yet straddling two worlds made me feel like a wishbone.

Lama couldn't solve my crisis of faith.

He had given me beautiful gifts: the gift of teachings on compassion and love, the gift of following the path earnestly and with a joyful heart. Now he was giving me the gift of letting me go. What direction should I turn? What would be my compass?

Voices

Lynne lingered in the living room after the other participants from the Project Compassion meeting left.

"How are you doing?" she asked, softly touching my shoulder.

"I'm exhausted, Lynne," I said. "My back hurts so badly I don't know what to do. I've gone to chiropractors, acupuncturists, stopped yoga, started yoga; you name it, I've tried it. I don't feel like I can carry all of this alone anymore."

Lynne listened thoughtfully. The exhilaration I felt when first starting Project Compassion was gone. I wanted the organization to succeed; I cared greatly about the mission. The divorce was taking more out of me than I expected; I just didn't have much time, money, or enthusiasm to give. How would I balance supporting my children and Project Compassion?

Ironically, at a time when I felt depleted by my role at Project Compassion, people would frequently tell me they were inspired by how I was living my "life purpose." During those conversations I would smile and say how "grateful I am to be a part of this great work." Which was true, but what I didn't say was that my heart was racing with fear—fear of failure, fear of the unknown, fear for my children's future. The external "show" and the internal conflict were starting to catch up with me. I began to question the price I was paying to maintain the image.

"You know what I think you should do?" Lynne said. "I think you should go lie down on your back, on the ground. Lie quietly with the intention that Mother Earth will support you."

She nodded her head with assurance, as if she were *positive* this would work. I envied Lynne's belief in her nature-based spirituality. And I was desperate enough and tired enough to try what I thought was a crazy suggestion.

A few days later I went to the one church that had consistently sustained me—the woods—and found a spot off of the path. Feeling self-conscious, I sat down and leaned back slowly, my hands pressing on the dirt and weeds for support. My back screamed with pain as I lowered myself down. Eventually I surrendered my body to the earth. Breathing deeply, I kept thinking, "I surrender this burden to you, Mother Earth; I open to your support." At first my mantra seemed stilted, but soon the reassuring rhythm moved effortlessly in me, "I surrender this burden to you, Mother Earth; I open to your support. I surrender this burden to you, Mother Earth; I open to your support."

Before I knew it I was crying small, muffled cries. Stopping briefly, I listened to a gust of wind high in the trees, but the tears soon returned. Spasms of deep, guttural, wracking sobs overtook me. When the fountain of my grief finally dried up I lay on my back, spent. I peered through the trees towering over me to the sky beyond and felt as if the shell around my hard heart had cracked.

Like the primitive woman, I felt the presence of Great Spirit all around me—in the bird's song, the rustling of the leaves, the smell of the earth, and the deep blue of the Carolina sky. In that moment I knew I was not alone—I was connected to the Sacred, and this bond would help me heal.

After my heart-opening experience I recommitted myself to spending time each day in meditation and prayer. Time alone in the woods reminded me of the support I could draw upon. Rekindling a lost sense of playfulness, I splurged on a purple leather journal cover with a funky brooch on the front. Journaling, reading spiritual books, and creating moments of sacred silence became like living water that quenched me and brought me back to life. As my strength returned, I also found a more centered perspective on my life.

I wondered if plowing wholeheartedly into Project Compassion had not only been a way to create meaning from losing Rhonda, but also a way to push away my grief. What about all this flipping out with Van? Had I focused on my anger with Van as a way to push away my pain of losing the dream of a "normal" family, and the loss of love? Had I been overconfident when I chose to become a single mom while nursing a non-profit in its infancy? Although my head and heart had wanted to ignore the attention my grief and exhaustion required, my body demanded I wake up; it actually woke me up with sleepless nights, backaches, and chronic bronchitis. Perhaps the weariness I felt at my own sheer bitchiness is what forced me to address the questions I tried to suppress.

Pushing the Boulder

A few weeks into my renewed morning ritual I wrote, "I can't seem to push this boulder called 'grief' all alone. I need more hands." I reached out to my friend Carol, a former hospice chaplain and Duke Divinity School graduate. We began meeting weekly for grief counseling, and I attended a grief support group. Even though two years had passed since Rhonda's death, I was surprised how frequently I wept, still. Carol's gentle, encouraging presence and soft, breathy voice tapped a well of sadness I had tried to cap. She helped me understand that my grief and anger were linked. Tending to one would diminish the other. Her stories, experiences, and mystical connection to the Divine showed me a new way of seeing and understanding all of the losses in my life. After months of meeting with Carol, I was ready to slow down and follow May Sarton's advice in the first stanza of her poem, "New Year Resolve":

The time has come
To stop allowing the clutter

To clutter my mind
Like dirty snow,
Shove it off and find
Clear time, clear water.

Carol helped me find a small retreat center south of Asheville to satisfy my craving for solitude. My sister, Anne, offered to come each day to give me a massage and Jin Shin Jyutsu, a form of healing touch. When I first arrived, I was shown to a small, second-floor room in a house behind the main house. Because I had broken my left foot a few weeks before, I couldn't easily maneuver the narrow stairway, and was relocated to the main house.

It seemed as though even my fifth metatarsal knew I needed rest. I had broken it when I slipped off a curb, rushing to pump gas while taking Kiki and Erin to camp. Here it was, one month later and I was on retreat; trying to read and pray, yet relegated to a loud room near the kitchen noises because of my broken foot. When Anne arrived with her massage table, she confirmed my sense that the setting was too busy for me. Even though the retreat leaders were warm and open women, I wanted to leave; but was afraid of offending my kind hosts. That evening at dinner there was a lively debate about Christian theology. Normally, I would find such a discussion energizing, but that night the talk seemed like irritating banter. After dinner, I pulled one of the leaders aside.

"Your home is lovely and you are all so kind, but something inside is calling for me to find even more seclusion than this. Would it be okay if I check out in the morning?"

"Of course it is. We'll help you with your bags after breakfast." Then she put a hand on each of my shoulders, "Mary, foster that 'voice' that's speaking to you," she said with a hint of fortune-teller.

Rocking Chair Revelation

The next day I drove north to Hendersonville, a quaint, trendy town in the foothills near Asheville. Downtown Hendersonville is somewhat schizophrenic. One of its personalities is affluent retiree, and the other is hippy artist. They coexist better than you might think. Walking on the sidewalk, I passed a young, dreadlock-crowned couple sipping coffee and drinking in each other's eyes; then a real estate office with a large window plastered with pictures of luxury cabins and homes for sale. Stopping in an upscale antique and garden store, I browsed at an uncharacteristically slow pace. A small, white garden statue of a young girl on a bench seemed sweet to me. I lingered over her, touching her. When I walked out of the store with my new statue in hand, I wondered how long it had been since I had taken time to enjoy.

Leaving town I drove leisurely, unconcerned about where I would land, and stumbled upon ten small, yellow cabins in the tiny, mountain town of Flat Rock. I knew immediately this was where I wanted to stay. I didn't want to go to a bed and breakfast, surrounded by lovers; but I didn't want to be secluded in a remote cabin either. This small clump of cabins was perfect. I pulled up in front of the office and opened my car door. The soothing smell of pine greeted me like a courteous doorman.

I walked into the office and was told I could have my pick of cabins; the place was nearly deserted. The next three days I spent sleeping, burning candles, receiving healing from Anne, writing in my journal, praying the rosary, sleeping, eating Häagen-Dazs ice cream bars, sleeping, driving into to town for long latte breaks, and sleeping some more.

After a couple of days of silence (except during Anne's visits), I was given a mysterious gift. Rocking in a rocking chair, journal on my lap, I enjoyed the steady, peaceful rain under the covered porch. Pressing my bare feet against the hard cement, moving back and forth, I thought of my grandmother's carport. The porch I was on and Grandma's carport both had green painted cement. I recalled rainy days at Grandma's house when my siblings and I would push each other up and down the ramp of the carport in Grandpa's wheelchair. More serene than I had felt in years, I began writing in my journal when I became aware of a mystical Presence nearby.

Heartened, I began a kind of free-form writing, "I have spent most of my adult life in a hurry. What the hell am I hurrying to? It is time to move to a different place. Oh yeah! Who am I? Why am I here? What do I want to accomplish with my remaining time on this earth? I am God's child. I know more than I am expressing. I am afraid of not fitting in, not being loved. I can be self-absorbed. Is this exercise self-discovery or self-absorption?

I began to write a dialogue with the unknown:

"Iliah, Elijah? What would happen if I weren't afraid?" came from within me.

"There would be great change. You are a daughter among many. You are ready," was the response from the unknown.

"How can I love more fully?" I asked.

"Drop the fear."

Then I felt the presence of my longtime supporter, Susan. She was close to both Rhonda and me in California. Even now it is difficult to explain what happened, but it was as if we were talking. I could hear her voice.

"She hears you," Susan's presence said. "She needs you to move on. You are ready."

"Will she still be with me?" I asked.

"Always," Susan said.

"I may never be loved like that again."

"Probably not."

Tears in my eyes, I continued to write. The rain and fog felt like a sacred shroud and the mystical Presence returned.

"You are ready; you are on your way out," the voice said, "out of the dark and into the light. You are sweeping it out. Take of the cup and drink."

I drew a crude chalice in my journal.

"The cup of life is always there. No need for distraction.

No need to quest on and on, just drink. Love your life, love your children, they are perfect in God's image and name. You do not need to fix them. Guide and love fully, drink fully. Embody kindness, forgiveness, and grace. From those comes compassion."

Then I felt like Rhonda was communicating with me.

"Drop the fucking agenda!" I wrote. "It will wear you out. Get Project Compassion out of your house. Your home is meant to be a sanctuary. You are a healing stop on the way. You are a catalyst for those who are ready. You learn from them and they from you."

I started to cry.

"I hate doing this without you!" I wrote

"You aren't. I am right there with you. Project Compassion has form. What we are doing, you and I, is beyond form. Don't be attached to it. Mother it, love it, and separate from it. Thank you. Thank you. I live on in you. You honor me. Remember what we wanted and needed. Don't get hung up on the form. Be there. Really be there.

"Just trust, just trust, Sweetie. You are so loved; you will be okay.... Light your candles, laugh, love your children—they will light your home. I am with you, Mary. You are more beautiful than you know."

I sat silently on the porch for a long time, listening to the rain and breathing in the cleansing pine scent.

Blazing a New Trail

As I packed up my things to leave the next day, I felt peaceful, renewed. I was clear, cleansed.

Back in Chapel Hill I knew that I needed to continue to provide opportunities for rest and clarity. My broken foot gave me an excuse to lie down on my bed and prop my foot on the pillow whenever I talked on the phone. Yet my work with Project Compassion still required a good deal of time—there were board meetings, lunches with donors, and committee meetings. I needed to decide how much time I was willing to give to this work.

Struggling with my role at Project Compassion reminded me of my final days with Rhonda. Both required me to discern which voice to attend to—my inner voice or external voices. Both experiences gave me the opportunity to let go in spite of the pressure to hold on. The external voices told me, "Who will fill the void? It is too early; you are still needed."

The inner voice told me, "Let go and trust that all will be well."

The external voices shouted, "Be afraid!"

I chose to follow the path that pulled at my heart, the path with an unhurried pace.

After prayerful consideration and counsel from friends, I decided to reduce my responsibilities at Project Compassion. The truth is, my health, my children's health, and Project Compassion's health depended on it.

***

My new perspective on life reminded me of the summer after I finished college, when I worked in Yellowstone National Park as a waitress. Although I had barely camped at all before my venture in Yellowstone, every weekend that summer I would pull my navy-blue backpack off the hook on the wall and fill it with just enough peanut butter, carrots, trail mix, coffee, and clothes to survive for a couple of days. My friends and I would gather, choose a challenging hike, and drive to the trailhead with our gear. At the beginning of each hike I felt the thrill of adventure along with a touch of fear. Would we encounter a grizzly? Would we be surprised by one of Yellowstone's dangerous and unpredictable lightning storms? Would we spot moose? Would this trail have beautiful wildflowers?

Those Yellowstone adventures introduced me to the empowering pulse of primitive woman. Her spirit seemed to flow through my veins as I hiked and explored. Something about my truth-telling journey re-awakened primitive woman in me. Yes, I was afraid. Yes, I was excited. Yes, I would survive. Yes there would be bears—and flowers—along the path.

It was time to claim who I was without all of the roles and labels that had previously defined me. It was time to blaze a new trail—traveling light, with a healthy respect for danger, and an unbridled sense of wonder. It was time to be independent and courageous. It was time to open myself directly to communion with Great Spirit and dance the sacred dance of life.

Part Four: Finding

"The beginning of wisdom is to call things by their right names."
—Chinese Proverb

Naming Me

Names are powerful. For my fortieth birthday, I decided to give myself a new one. I figured this decade-marking rite of passage was a good time to start using it.

When I was a little girl—except when my older siblings chased me around teasing, "Mary Bea the bumble bee"—I loved being called Mary Bea. As a teenager, I shed the Bea and admonished careless family members who "forgot" to simply call me Mary. My parents were the only people on earth still allowed to call me Mary Bea with impunity.

When I married Van, I struggled with letting go of my maiden name—Krohn. I didn't want to lose my heritage, yet I wanted to share my new husband's name. I completed the Social Security form to be Mary Beatrice Meyer, when my new card came I didn't like how I had lost the name Krohn. I returned to the office, filled out the form to become Mary Beatrice Krohn-Meyer, but found the hyphenated name cumbersome. Finally, I settled on using my maiden name, Krohn, as my middle name, and taking my husband's last name. Over time, I adjusted to my new name, Mary Krohn Meyer, but having dropped Beatrice, I always felt like I had given up a piece of me.

Who Would I Become?

Impending divorce was changing everything. I didn't want to wear the family name of someone I was no longer married to, but my maiden name no longer fit, either. I was a different person from who I was when I was married and when I was as a child. If I no longer related to Mary Meyer, and I would no longer be Mary Krohn, who then would I become?

I was self-conscious about my dramatic and unconventional

thoughts. I felt like a part of me wanted to be born, and I was apprehensive that this new me wasn't willing to play it safe. "Now what?" I asked myself. I had already taken enough risks in the last few years; what other changes could possibly be awaiting me? I kept my naming thoughts to myself for months, until one night my friend Becky created the safe space for me to share my secret.

Becky is a mystic who favors flowing, purple skirts and unconventional spirituality. She's one of those rare friends you can say absolutely anything to and know there will be no judgment—rare indeed. Sensitive to my many nights as a single person, Becky made herself available for an occasional evening together. On one of those occasions, we sat under the large tree in her small backyard and enjoyed a gin and tonic.

"So what plans are you making for your fortieth birthday ?" Becky asked.

"How did you know I was obsessing about this? Girl, you are a mind reader."

"Well, who wouldn't be? Turning forty is a rite of passage, you know."

"This rite of passage is going to go relatively unnoticed." I said. "I have already worn my friends out with enough divorce drama. I really don't want any more attention. I don't even want a fortieth birthday party."

She flashed a grin and said, "We can't have that!"

"Okay," I said. "Here's the deal. I don't want a big hoopla, but I do want to change my name for my fortieth birthday." Lubricated by the gin and feeling safe in Becky's home, I let my secret tumble out. Psychic Becky probably knew already.

"Well of course you do, dear. What will it be?" Becky asked.

"I don't even know for sure. I want to keep Mary. I want to take back my middle name which is Beatrice. I was named after my Aunt Bea."

I leaned back in the plastic lawn chair and stared up at the hazy, starless summer sky. "I just don't know what my last name will be."

"Do you want to look at the cards?" Becky said, her lips curling up in a scandalous grin.

"Sure," I said. "Awesome idea."

We moved inside to begin our work. Sitting at a wooden table in her hallway, I chose a tarot deck from her drawerful of colorful cards.

"So," I began. "I'm not who I was."

Giving voice to this unspoken desire unleashed unexpected ideas and emotions. I told her about wanting to honor my mother's Irish heritage; that since I was a little girl, I had identified more with my Irish than my German roots. I felt like the first forty years of my life had been defined by masculine, patriarchal choices. My choice to forgo a political science major was made to please my father, who thought a business major would offer me more possibilities. My choice to pursue a financial planning career was driven by a desire to make lots of money. My choice to move frequently to promote Van's career was driven by a desire to "stand by my man."

These were good choices at the time, but all choices of the head. I wanted to give more voice to my heart. Krohn came to me by birth; Meyer by marriage. Who did I want to birth now? What name would signify this union of the head and the heart? Becky listened devoutly.

Rummaging through a drawer, she found a piece of paper and pen. For the first time, I wrote down the names I was considering. Talking and writing at the same time, I blurted out, "My mother's maiden name is Todd, I love the name Mary Todd, but there's that whole Mary Todd Lincoln thing."

Becky nodded, "Go on."

"Her mother's maiden name is Sullivan. I have lots of aunts and uncles who are Sullivans. Three of these Sullivan sisters I knew quite well growing up. I admired their independence and political savvy," I said. "They were way ahead of their time and lived well into their nineties. I liked them, even if two of them were a little pissy sometimes."

We laughed. "How so?" Becky asked.

"Oh man, my Aunt Bea was a sharp cookie, and she could be sharp-tongued. Maybe because she never had kids, she used to scrunch her face up and look so disgusted when we did the least little thing wrong. Honestly, I admired and feared that woman!

"I remember hearing that she continued to end her day with a cocktail even when she was moved to an assisted living facility that forbade alcohol. I bet those aides were afraid to mess with her!"

I signed the names:

Mary Beatrice Todd
Mary Beatrice Sullivan

"Would it be too weird if I changed my first name to include Mary Bea?" I wondered out loud. "I remember when someone at work did that—changed her first name. I thought it was pretty odd; we all snickered behind her back. We laughed out loud when she changed it back! I don't know if I have the courage to do that. Also, I don't want to put everybody through that whole first name change thing."

"Maybe worrying about what other people think isn't what this name is about," Becky suggested. "Maybe it's time you give worrying about what everybody thinks a rest."

We talked some more and Becky read my cards. It was almost midnight by the time we finished. As the day came to a close, I was surprisingly comfortable that whatever name I chose would represent who I was becoming. I began to believe that whatever was continuing to grow within me was worthy of being nurtured, loved, and named. Over the course of the next few days I kept signing "Mary B. Sullivan," "Mary Bea Sullivan," "Mary

Sullivan" on scraps of paper. In an effort to honor my father's heritage and to give birth to what I was becoming, I chose Mary Beatrice Krohn Sullivan.

Telling Family

Brendan and Kiki ran into the kitchen. The sweat mixed with dirt on their faces was evidence of a fun day at summer camp. They took their seats at the table and I placed their plates in front of them.

"I want to talk to you about something important. I want you to know that you can say anything you want to about what I'm about to tell you." I said. "It's important for me to know how you really feel. Also, if you need time to think about it, that's okay too."

Brendan's forehead wrinkled, tight and worried. Kiki lifted her head and searched my face eagerly for a clue.

"I'm thinking of changing my last name. One of the things I'm concerned about is that it might be hard for you. You know how Susan has a different last name than Ross, Adam, and Chris?"

They both nodded.

"That's how it would be. You would still be Brendan and Kiki Meyer, but I would be Mary Sullivan. I might do it for my fortieth birthday instead of waiting for the divorce to be final in the winter."

"Sullivan? Why Sullivan?" Brendan asked.

"Good question."

I explained.

"Plus, I think it's pretty—Mary Sullivan."

"It seems a little weird," Brendan said.

"I think it's kinda cool," Kiki encouraged. I wasn't sure if her positive response was genuine, or a knee-jerk reaction to disagree with her brother.

"It's so important to me that both of you are comfortable with this," I said. "That you know it doesn't affect anything about us as a family, just my name will change." I wanted desperately for them to be okay with this, yet another change. "I've thought about it a long time. It's not that I think your dad is a bad guy or anything, but if we aren't married, it's kinda hard for me to keep using his name. But I know it's your name too. At school and sports and everything, it might be uncomfortable having a mom with a different last name—especially since it didn't used to be that way. I want to know what you think about the whole thing. Like I said, you can take some time."

We picked at our food and after a few minutes, Brendan surprised me.

"It'll be hard sometimes, Mom, but I don't think it's that big of a deal. I mean if that's what you wanna do, you should do it."

"I think it's pretty cool. So how do you change your name? Like, can I change mine from Kristin to Kiki so that I don't have to tell all my teachers my nickname at the beginning of every year?"

***

When I called my mother and told her about my new name, she cried tears of gratitude, perhaps because of generations of unclaimed honor. She shared Sullivan stories, and I listened with new ears. I was afraid to tell my dad. I didn't want him to think I was diminishing his importance in my life. I didn't want to insult his family name. No one in my family had ever done anything remotely like this before; I wondered how he would respond.

I wanted to break the news to Dad in person so I drove to Florida and spent a week alone with my parents while Brendan and Kiki were with their dad. Every day I thought, "Today I will speak to Dad." Every night I went to bed without bringing it up.

On the last evening of the trip, my mom announced, "Dave, Mary has something important to talk about. Would you make some of your great margaritas and we'll all go down to the beach?"

Wide-eyed, I looked at my mom as if to say, "Whoa, you aren't really going to 'out' me are you?"

She looked me straight in the eye as if to say, "Yeah! Wimp!"

We sat on our beach chairs an hour or so before sunset. It was a gorgeous July day and we had enjoyed a restful, loving, fun week together.

"Umm, aaaaahh, I just wanted you to know that I'm going to change my name," I said, leaning forward in my chair nervously running my hand through the sand.

There was no reaction from Dad. He stared out at the ocean and clanked the ice in his glass.

"At first I was thinking Mary Krohn, but ummm, ummm, the more I think about it, I really like the name Mary Sullivan. You know, after Grandma Todd's family?" I was bumbling this in a big way. Was I turning forty or four?

No comment. Dad's face remained stoic.

"Anyway, it's not like I don't like the name Krohn, it's just that I wanted to move toward Sullivan."

Dad nodded.

"You know I really like these new investment guys that Dave turned me on to in Boston," he said.

Exasperated, mom leaned forward in her chair and shook Dad's knee, "Dave, your daughter just said something important to you. What do you think?" She stared him down, letting him know we weren't going anywhere until he answered.

"I think my daughter is an adult and she wants to change her name. That's what I think."

Relieved, astonished, I shook my head, grinning. My eyes scanned the horizon as the waves gently rolled into the shore, the evening sky casting gorgeous orange, red, yellow shadows on the water.

Crystal Box

In honor of Mom's seventieth birthday, all of my brothers and sisters, along with their spouses and children, gathered at my home in Chapel Hill. Prior to the whole gang arriving, Mom, Kiki, and I celebrated our seventieth, tenth, and fortieth birthdays together. These three momentous birthdays happened within a week of each other. To honor the occasion, we had a photographer take our picture on my front lawn, and we dined at Magnolia Grill, one of Durham's finest restaurants, in beautiful new dresses. That evening, grandmother, mother, and daughter collectively and ceremoniously said good-bye to one decade and hello to another. The black and white photograph of the three of us is displayed prominently in our home and in Mom's as a treasured memento.

Frequently, I tell my mother, "I'm glad I'm in your gene pool!" I don't know if most daughters feel this way, but I think my mother is beautiful, inside and out. Mom is four inches shorter than me, so hugging requires bending over. She is blessed with youthful, Irish skin, gorgeous hazel eyes, and currently, her hair is blonde. When I thought of growing my own gray hair out, Mom's comment was, "I can't possibly have a daughter who is gray!" Mom's most beautiful feature is her smile, which she shares generously.

The night of Mom's party there were at least twenty-five of us on the deck overlooking the woods. As is usually the case when my family gathers, the event was loud, rowdy, and joke-filled. Never missing an opportunity to kid, my brothers ribbed me about my new name.

"Who are you again?"

Self-conscious, I chuckled with them.

Under a blanket of stars, surrounded by her beloved family, Mom was beaming. After she had opened all of her gifts, kissed every child, grandchild, and great-grandchild, she clapped her hands together, turned to me and pointed her finger.

"Now, I have something for you! Dave, hand me the

package."

My father handed her a small beautifully wrapped gift that she in turn passed to me. Mom was excited and the glow in her eyes said, "This is something special."

I began to unveil the heavy package. Each tear revealed a little more of the gift. First, a corner of clear glass or crystal came into view. Then I saw that it was rectangular, cut with a Waterford-like pattern. Finally, I realized I was clasping a crystal jewelry box. Holding the box close to the porch light so I could inspect it further, I choked up as I read out loud the engraving on the lid: "Mary Beatrice Sullivan, August 7, 2002."

Out in Public

The final step in my transformation to Mary Sullivan was my trip to the Carrboro Division of Motor Vehicles office to change my driver's license. When my number was finally called, I approached the government-grade metal desk and sat down. Across from me was a woman who could have been a caricature from a 1950s movie. Dressed in the official blue DMV uniform, she had brown shoulder-length hair slicked close to her head that flipped up at the ends (I could imagine the huge pink curlers). I handed her the legal document indicating my name change.

"Divorce or marriage?" She asked as she looked up from her paperwork.

"Divorce," I mumbled.

She smiled, "I thought so. They're usually the happy ones!"

I answered her humor with a grateful smile. After taking my picture, she instructed me to wait in a chair across the room.

"Mary Sullivan," she called. My new name filled the air of the DMV and I liked the sound of it.

Walking over to the metal desk, I was shocked as she took my old driver's license, stared straight at me, and dramatically threw it behind her back, into the trash can.

"Out with Mary Meyer!" she bellowed. Laughing, I put my hand out for my new license as she said, "in with Mary Sullivan."

Riding Toward My Future

I sprinted down the garage steps with my arms outstretched, thrilled to have a kid-free weekend and a day off of work. I had found a paying job. Getting it required help from my father, and it was with a risky start-up operation, but I was desperate and am a gambler by nature. Fortunately, the salary was what I hoped for and I was able to work from home, which meant I was available for the kids after school.

Project Compassion was in great hands—and they weren't mine. Providence prevailed, Project Compassion rallied from its own near-death experience and the board raised enough money to hire a full-time executive director. James Brooks, the hospice chaplain I had met at Care Team training, showed an interest in returning to his native North Carolina. The board was wowed by his experience and enthusiasm. I still held the title of board chair, but James was running the day-to-day operations masterfully.

I pushed my blue mountain bike up and off its hook on the garage wall. Cobwebs, tangled in the spokes, clung to my hands. As I rolled the bike down the driveway, the auburn, gold, and brown of fall beckoned me to play. I felt like a little girl again, the one who used to leap into piles of newly-raked leaves. Once on my bike, I pulled my fleece pullover down in the back, hoping it covered most of my butt. Biking shorts were no longer flattering. Okay, honestly, they have never been flattering. I made a silent vow never to be friends with anyone who looked good in biking shorts, and started riding.

In just two miles I reached a road aptly named Dairyland. Riding past the rolling hills and picturesque dairy farms soothed my overworked body. Even though my legs and heart pumped fast, with each mile I dropped into a deeper, more meditative state. Thoughts of faxes and emails gave way to, well …nothing. I turned right on Union Church Grove Road, breathing hard up the long hills and coasting fast on the down steep slopes. Finally, I turned around to head home and noticed a "For Sale" sign pointing down a road off of Dairyland. Enjoying the luxury of free time, I explored a little more.

There was a small horse farm at the entrance of the neighborhood. The lots seemed to be at least an acre each, and no two homes looked alike. One was a light blue Victorian, another red brick; many had wraparound porches. I rode up to the home with the "For Sale" sign in front and gasped, "No way. No way." Before Van and I separated, I had drawn a rough sketch of the house I would like to move into as a single woman. The house I sketched in my journal was cozy, with a wraparound porch, and situated on a large, wooded lot. And here I was, staring at the likeness, in real life.

I pulled my cell phone out of my pullover pocket and called my real estate agent, Lucia. There should be a special category of sainthood for real estate agents who work with the newly-separated. One day I wanted to sell the big house and "be rid of it." The next I would cry, "How can I uproot my children at a time like this?" Lucia had patiently listened to all of my worries and my dreams. She weathered multiple false starts. I would fill out the paperwork to put the house on the market, only to pull back because I wasn't ready yet.

A divorcée herself, she repeatedly reminded me, "I would have never become a successful businesswoman if I didn't have to make it on my own. You'll be fine and you'll find out you can do more than you ever thought you could."

As with many of my relationships at that time, I knew I was receiving more than I gave.

"Lucia, I think I'm standing in front of my next house."

"What's the address?" she asked. "I'll look it up."

I gave her the address and heard her clicking fingers sail

across the keyboard. She rattled off details from the multiple listing, "Three bedrooms, fenced one-acre lot, master on the first floor."

I couldn't believe the price. Driving a couple of extra miles into town would be worth the savings in mortgage.

"I want a showing," I said. "I want to see it."

"Okay, I'll see how soon we can get in and call you back."

A few days later we went inside the house. Recently painted in sages, yellows, and creams, the inside oozed serenity. Within a week we had agreed on a price. I put my home on the market. Van and I were communicating more effectively, and he even agreed to move into the big house if it took too long to sell. I wanted to trust that all would be well, but I was also terrified at taking such big leaps on my own, for the first time in my life.

Piña Coladas

Two months later, my first single-parent Christmas was just around the corner. The big house hadn't sold and I was closing on the cute, small house before the New Year. Knowing that I was potentially on the verge of balancing multiple mortgages and feeling guilty about the divorce, I did what any self-respecting mom would do. I borrowed money and took the kids to Cancun. Actually, in self defense, I had been planning the trip before I decided to buy the cute, small house, and didn't have the heart to cancel it.

Even though I knew better than to go in hock for a vacation, something inside me knew the kids and I really needed to go somewhere and have fun together. Now I could better understand one of Rhonda's controversial decisions—to travel to Hawaii with her family at an unlikely, and some thought foolish, time. I felt driven to prove to Brendan and Kiki, to me, and to the world that we were a "normal" family. I wanted my children to know that just because mommy and daddy didn't live together anymore, we could go on living. As crazy as it was, and even though this choice would add to my financial stress when we returned, it was one of the best decisions I have ever made. Kiki and Brendan still talk about going to Cancun as one of the greatest times of their lives.

It didn't start out so well. When we first arrived, Brendan came running over to me after checking out the pool.

"Mom, they have virgin piña coladas here and the guy brings them to you at your chair! Can I get one?" He pleaded. "Can I wait for you by the pool and get one?"

"Oh my God! Do you think we came here to spend a bunch of money on drinks by the pool?" I grabbed both Brendan and Kiki by the arm and turned them toward me.

"Look, both of you need to understand; we're lucky to be here. I can't go wasting a bunch of money on stupid things like expensive drinks, okay?"

"Okay!" Brendan barked back, making a nasty face before running away.

That night, I couldn't sleep because I was calculating in my head how long it would take for me to pay for this trip. Worried that the house wouldn't sell and that I had been terribly foolish to borrow money for such an extravagant vacation, I cried while the kids slept. I sat up in bed and was startled by the glow of the night light shining on Brendan and Kiki's faces. They looked incredibly beautiful, happy, and for the first time in a year, peaceful. Somewhere during the divorce, I had disconnected from Brendan and Kiki and hadn't even known it.

At that moment I realized that all of the worrying in the world wouldn't change anything. For better or worse, I had decided to make the trip, we were *on* the trip, and it was up to me to choose if I would enjoy the trip. If I wasn't careful, I would squander this opportunity to fulfill the promise that this adventure held for the three of us.

The next day, we rode the bus to a water amusement park. Brendan and Kiki were so excited they could barely sit still in their seats. When we reached the park, we emptied our belongings into a locker.

"Can we go swim with the dolphins first?" Brendan asked.

"Sure," I replied. We followed the dolphin-shaped arrows until we reached a wooden walkway leading a hundred yards or so out into the ocean. We walked up to the booth at the base of the walkway where we were given yellow life vests. Brendan and Kiki sprinted ahead. I walked fast, trying to catch up.

Six dolphins swam in a large enclosed area. From a small platform, a fit, blonde trainer in a black wetsuit blew his whistle, commanding the dolphins to jump in unison. All six dolphins burst above the surface of the water, arching playfully in the air, then plunged back under the surface. Brendan whipped his head around toward me; his huge brown eyes and brilliant smile grabbed me.

The trainer encouraged us to climb down the ladder backwards into the water. The dolphins circled the eight of us in our group. We were instructed how to properly approach the dolphins to pet them. Suddenly, there was a squeal from Kiki and I protectively swam toward her.

"That was soooo cool, mom!" Kiki said.

"What was?"

"One of the dolphins just touched me. I could feel its skin. It's so smooth and silky," she giggled.

I looked over at Brendan. He was swimming sideways trying to catch one of the dolphins. The way he pursued and reached out to the dolphin reminded me of when he was in kindergarten and our black labrador, Boomer, was a puppy. Brendan would run behind and reach out for that puppy every chance he could. It had been a long time since I had seen Brendan reach out for anything and trust that it would be okay.

For the next fifteen minutes we swam with the dolphins. We rode on their backs, received kisses from them, and petted them as they swam by. There was a primal freedom in swimming so close to "wild" animals. The high-pitched calls of the dolphins seemed to pierce through our pain. Our session concluded with the dolphins jumping in the air again, only this time we were in the water with them and could feel the waves splashing in our faces. The trainer suggested we clap to reward them. Brendan and Kiki kept on clapping and laughing well after the show was over. Finally we swam to the ladder, slicing through the water, mimicking the dolphins' dives.

We rode water rides that day, running and squealing from one attraction to the next. Even though I resisted, the kids enticed me to go with them down a huge waterslide in an oversized inner tube. Afterwards, they imitated the way I had screamed before the ride even started. We hiked up the ladder and rode that ride at least five more times, screaming only a little less each time.

The following day I was lying on the beach watching Brendan and Kiki splashing in the crystal blue-green water. Gazing at them in the bright sun, I shaded my eyes with my hand. My children were laughing and body surfing together. I marveled at these two precious beings. What a gift that they were healthy, in my life, and they loved and enjoyed each other.

"Mom, come in and swim!" Kiki yelled.

I walked to the water's edge, and then playfully ran, parting white droplets of ocean in the sun. The three of us bobbed up and down, waiting for just the right wave to ride. At one point, I dunked under the water and emerged, nose first, plastering my wet hair back with my hands. When I opened my eyes, Brendan and Kiki were springing out of the water too, smiling in our Caribbean baptismal font.

I encouraged the kids to stay and play when I returned to my beach chair. Content, I closed my eyes and soaked up the luxury of warmth and peace that seemed to be radiating from the sun. Sitting up, I waved for *el camarero* and ordered one real and two virgin piña coladas.

Sleepless

When we returned from Mexico, my sense of anxiety returned.

One particular night, the clock was not my friend. I was sleep-deprived, but I couldn't sleep. Awakened yet again, I checked the time—3:00 a.m. Tossing to my right side, I scrunched my eyes shut, hoping for sleep. No luck, 3:15. I turned to my left side and pulled the covers over my head. No luck, 3:45. Finally I flung the sheets off and began my unwelcome 4:00 a.m. ritual. Pulling on my robe, slipping into my fuzzy slippers, I shuffled down the hall to make myself a latte.

Trying to tune out the never-ending buzz in my head, I grabbed one of the afghan blankets Rhonda made and swaddled myself in it. Sighing, I settled into my favorite, yellow chair with my latte, folded my legs underneath me, leaned over to grab my journal and waited for the familiar twang from the springs underneath me—a sort of "chair scolding" for using it as it was intended.

Looking out the window, I saw only the darkness of night. Even though I knew the woods were outside, I couldn't see them. Neither could I see what I was doing to perpetuate my lingering feelings of anger and resentment. Words poured onto the pages of my journal. I let my latte turn bitter and cold from neglect.

I craved a sustained return of the creative, loving energy that had brought joy to me and those around me. I wanted to move forward in a more peaceful way. I prayed for my heart to soften. I prayed for relief from anger's co-conspirator, anguish. I prayed for peace in my heart and in my home.

The darkness outside lifted slightly and I could barely make out the silhouettes of the trees. I continued writing. The same surreal feeling that had enveloped me the night Rhonda died returned. Again, even though it was my hand moving across the page, the words seemed to come from beyond me.

Releasing, Releasing, Releasing
Anger, fear, resentment
Jealousy, pride and hurt

A cocktail of confusion
Set upon personal destruction
Sapping energy from creative force

Opening, loving, caring
Where in the soul do you reside
Pastor, mentor, lover, come home, come home

I read the strange poem over and over and over again. Most of it made sense, but the last line seemed bizarre. "Pastor, mentor, lover, come home, come home"—what did that mean? Perhaps they were words from me to me. Perhaps I was calling me home.

I set my journal on the coffee table and closed my eyes. Placing my right hand on my heart I took a few deep breaths and prayed for my heart to soften. I desperately wanted to lighten my load. My anger had been stealing all my energy, energy that was needed to find a new, harmonious way of being. Feeling my heart beat beneath my hand, I imagined that crucial muscle softening with each new beat. At first it was difficult to sit still with my turbulent emotions. Dark waves of grief washed over me. Rhonda, my marriage, security—so much had been lost in so little time. Eventually, the intensity of my sadness subsided and a glint of warmth radiated from my heart throughout my body.

Dancing Naked Under the Moon

Part Five: Loving

"Love, like a river, will cut a new path whenever it meets an obstacle."
—Crystal Middlemas

Pastor, Mentor, Lover, Come Home, Come Home

The very next day I was standing in my closet, looking for something to wear that didn't say, D-E-S-P-E-R-A-T-E, but was also cute and sexy. The pile of rejected clothes strewn on my bed displayed my anxiety. In a few hours I would be picking up Malcolm Marler, who was flying in from Birmingham to the Raleigh airport. He was returning to Chapel Hill to facilitate Care Team training. Everything leading up to our meeting had been strictly business, yet I felt that old pull of possibility and a flutter of excitement. Finally, standing in front of the mirror, I decided to wear a long-sleeved white top, red suede vest, tan pants, and brown boots.

I was nervous about being alone in a car and out to dinner with a single man for the first time in decades. I had not dated during my thirteen-month separation. Before entering a relationship with someone else, I wanted to get to know myself better. Standing in front of the mirror, trying to suck in my tummy, I thought, "Girl, you were twenty-one years younger and ten pounds lighter the last time you went on a date!"

"Wait," I told myself, "this is not a date!"

Ever since Project Compassion had hired James, I was thankfully free from managing details for events like Care Team training. However, I had volunteered to pick Malcolm up at the airport under the pretense of freeing James up to tend to logistics. My girlfriend Mindy, who had met Malcolm at the last training, encouraged me to spend time with him on this trip. Mindy was concerned about how long I was taking to return to the dating world and suggested that a sweet, out-of-town guy was a safe way to start.

Beginnings

This would be my third meeting with Malcolm. The first was when I had attended Care Team training in Birmingham a few years before. The second time had been only eight months before when Malcolm and Carol Padgett came to Chapel Hill to facilitate training for Project Compassion.

For some reason this man, whom I had seen as a nice chaplain when I first met him in Alabama, looked and felt different to me during our second encounter. I remember it vividly. Malcolm had been wearing a black turtleneck sweater and pleated dress pants. His strong chest and arm muscles were visible through his turtleneck. When I greeted him he smiled and I wondered, "Why hadn't I noticed those gorgeous blue eyes before?"

At the training, I had been impressed with Malcolm's facilitation skills, the way he gently coaxed the participants to tell their stories, the way he listened intently and smiled often. I was drawn to the paradoxes of this man, who was strong and masculine yet caring and feminine. I had laughed at his jokes and even found myself flirting with him when I borrowed his phone at the break.

At the end of that first day of training I had hosted a dinner for Malcolm, James, and Carol. While I sliced the carrots, leeks, and mushrooms to accompany the salmon I was preparing, Malcolm had leaned against the counter, keeping me company. I smiled as he told about his old football days at Clemson. We stayed in the kitchen chatting while Carol and James sat on the back porch. As I finished preparing the meal, I noticed a familiar look in Malcolm's eye and thought, "That preacher boy is checking me out!" Shockwaves ran through my body.

Later the four of us sat out on the back porch overlooking the woods. As the evening wore on, our energy shifted from the intensity of the training to the relaxed enjoyment of each other's company. The warm spring air was a welcome change from the stuffiness of the conference room. Cicadas and crickets serenaded us. I was struck by Malcolm's melodic voice and southern mannerisms. He gently petted Boomer, who surrendered his big, black head into Malcolm's hand and groaned when he stroked his ear.

Malcolm spoke about his years of walking with people during times of great loss. "My purpose is to create community and connection for people when they need it most," he said as he grabbed a peanut from the dish. Something about his confident clarity caught my attention. I was captivated as he told us of fulfilling his lifelong dream of building a house on Alabama's Smith Lake. A twinge of sadness swept through me when he discussed his girlfriend and their potential plans to marry.

The next day, at the conclusion of the training, we all stood in a circle and held hands. I was next to Malcolm and liked the way he held my hand—firmly, but gently. I thanked Malcolm and Carol for the training and turned to hug each of them. When Malcolm and I embraced, he wrapped his strong arms around me. I felt safe, but not suffocated.

My friend, a different Carol, who attended the training, later said to me, "There was electricity between you two that was hot!" I remember enjoying that brief embrace and feeling a bit embarrassed that we may have lingered too long.

Natural Disasters

Malcolm and I next spoke six months later. Chapel Hill had experienced a horrific ice storm that knocked down trees, power lines, and telephone lines. Much of North Carolina was immobilized and we had been without power for four days, living in the silence that comes when refrigerators no longer hum and heaters aren't heating.

There was nothing maternal about Mother Nature's grand finale to the ice storm—gripping cold below twenty degrees. Even when we were indoors our fingers turned red. The kids and I had fun playing board games by candlelight and building fires. Sleeping was not fun. In a variation of the "three-dog night" scenario, Brendan brought his mattress down to my room and placed it next to the bed Kiki and I shared to keep warm. Boomer and Daisy curled up on Brendan's mattress.

"I can see my breath," Kiki said, lying next to me in bed.

"That is not a good thing," I replied, laughing.

At the end of those four days, the phone rang, cutting through the silence. I was so excited that the telephone worked, I practically yelled, "Hey there!"

"Hi, this is Malcolm Marler in Alabama." He sounded surprised by my tone. "I just wanted to check up on you because I heard Chapel Hill was covered in ice."

"Oh hi, Malcolm. This is the first phone call I've been able to receive for days! We're hanging in there. You're so thoughtful to call."

"Well, my lake house was hit by a tornado a few weeks ago and I find I'm more sensitive to how these disasters can be difficult for folks."

I stretched out on my bed as we caught up on the comings and goings of the last half-year. The view out my window could have been a Currier and Ives Christmas card—a male cardinal perched on an icy Leyland Cypress branch. It felt great to have an adult conversation, with an adult male, no less. We spoke comfortably.

"How did the wedding go?" I asked.

"Actually, it didn't. I decided if I had to convince myself to get married, I probably shouldn't do it. We broke up the same week my home was hit by the tornado. It was like experiencing a tornado inside and out."

"Oh. I'm so sorry," I said. "I can't imagine trying to handle both of those tragedies at the same time."

"It's okay. It really is for the better. It's just hard." Malcolm continued, "I'm finding the tornado is a good metaphor for what's going on inside of me too. It's overwhelming if I think about everything at once, so I just make a list each day and check off what gets done. I'm taking it one day at a time. People have been great. My neighbors are letting me drive down their driveway because mine is covered in trees. They are teaching me how to use a chainsaw so I can clear away some of this mess. I can tell you one thing, I'm learning a lot."

We shifted gears and started to discuss the training he was going to offer in a couple of months.

"I'm looking forward to seeing you again in January," I said. "If you want to stay in town an extra day or so I could give you a little tour of the Durham–Chapel Hill area," I added. Not sure exactly what I was offering or why I was doing it, I surprised myself by this impulsive gesture.

"Thanks, but I think I'll fly right back. I'm flying all over the country now and have a lot to do, so I'll probably want to come home for the weekend," he replied.

Ouch! I felt my cheeks redden. Pressing the heel of my palm into my forehead, I hoped my voice didn't expose my disappointment and embarrassment. What was I thinking? What was I offering?

"That makes sense. Well, I'll see you in a couple of months. Even though you're going through some hard stuff, I hope you have a good Christmas."

"You too, Mary. I hope everything's okay with your house."

Airport Pick-Up

Three months had passed and now I was driving to the airport, a little nervous and anxious to see Malcolm again. He was waiting underneath the Southwest Airlines sign wearing a white turtleneck, khakis, and a leather bomber jacket. Leaning against his red overnight bag, he looked relaxed. He smiled and waved when he saw me. I pulled over and jumped out of the car to give him a hug as he put his luggage in the back. At 5 feet 8 inches tall, Malcolm is only a couple of inches taller than me. I liked how I fit just under his broad shoulders. To my surprise, he gushed, "You look great!"

I smiled and we both got into the car. The energy between us pulsed red hot from the moment we hugged.

As we drove away from the airport, sheets of rain beat down on the car. I had intended to walk with Malcolm through Duke University's gardens before we went to dinner. Clearly, that plan wasn't going to work. Trying to come up with a new agenda, I suggested that we tour Duke Chapel. Malcolm liked the idea. Duke Chapel was a beautiful, stone, gothic-style building, built in the 1930s, with a prominent front tower over 200 feet tall and seating for more than 1,600 people.

I would have been no more surprised if the angel Gabriel had swooped down and opened my door than I was when the notoriously tough Duke Chapel traffic officers allowed us to park illegally so we wouldn't have to run far in the rain. We dashed up the steps and Malcolm held the heavy wooden door open for me. We entered together. After admiring the stained glass, woodwork, and stone, I looked at Malcolm.

"I love to sit in silence in churches. Would you mind if we just sat for a moment?"

"I'd like that."

We slid into one of the long, wooden pews near the front and to the right of the altar. Sitting in complete silence, we were close enough that I could feel his arm next to mine. A wave of peace that defied reason passed through me. Eyes closed, breathing in the earthy smell of his leather coat, I felt safe. The silence that surrounded us seemed sacred. From a mysterious place deep inside me came a commanding thought: *I want him to hold me and never let go*. I was startled by my unexpected thought, but continued to sit quietly. Again, the thought *I want him to hold me and never let go* reverberated through me.

After a little while, I opened my eyes and saw that Malcolm still had his eyes closed. Opening his eyes he gazed at the ornate altar and then turned toward me.

"Are you ready to go?" he said, smiling gently.

"Sure. Thank you, this was nice."

"It was nice," Malcolm said. "So peaceful—a great idea."

When he stood up, Malcolm stepped out of the pew and backed up so I could exit in front of him. As we left, he opened the door for me and gently placed his hand on my back. I felt honored, holy, and sexy all at once.

We drove toward Chapel Hill to eat at a trendy, new restaurant near Franklin Street. Halfway to Chapel Hill I thought, "I don't want to run into anyone who knows me tonight."

"I think I'm going to head back to Durham," I said. "The more I think of it there's a great place there I've never been to we can try."

"I'm game. It'll all be new to me."

The electrical, magical feel of the afternoon carried through dinner. We spent hours talking after our plates had been cleared away. At one point, he placed his hand on the table and I thought, *that is a beautiful hand*. Looking into his blue eyes I thought, *those are beautiful eyes*. Listening to him describe the pain of losing his father, I knew, *this is a beautiful heart*. We talked about our lives, our loves, our dreams.

"I loved the woods that were along the driveway before the tornado hit," he said. "FEMA actually took more than thirty truckloads of fallen trees away from my property."

"I can't believe that. I can't even imagine what that would look like."

"Well, I'm trying to decide what I can do with that land now that it's cleared. That part is probably half an acre. You've had a horse before—is that enough room for a horse?"

I was inspired by his positive spirit.

Later, he confided, "One of my life's greatest heartbreaks is not having children. I hope to get that chance one day."

Having taken years of yoga, I had often heard references

to “opening your heart chakra.” That night, I physically felt the sensation of my heart opening. Looking at Malcolm, listening to Malcolm, my chest seemed to be breaking open and exploding. The sensation of heat pulsed in me. Taking Malcolm’s courageous lead, I found myself exposing hopes and dreams I usually kept well protected inside.

“I think I’m a wild, western woman at heart. My dream is to own a small horse farm in Montana some day.”

My body followed my heart. Desire that had been dormant lifted her head and awoke. When we walked out onto the sidewalk after our evening, Malcolm leaned over and kissed me. Stunned, I thought, “This is my first kiss as a single woman.” I looked at him and blushed. When we reached his hotel, saying our good-byes in the car, I boldly, unexpectedly leaned over and planted a great big kiss on his mouth.

Over the next few days we stole every moment together that we could find. Creating that time required ingenuity because I actually moved into my new home the day after our first dinner together, and Malcolm’s schedule was packed with commitments for Project Compassion events. Somehow, we knew that we wanted to see more of each other, even after Malcolm returned to Alabama. I wasn’t sure we could stay connected given the nearly 600 miles that separated our homes. Malcolm was undaunted.

“I’m flying so much now that I have a lot of free Southwest tickets,” he said. “If I send you a ticket, would you come to the lake next weekend when your kids are with their dad?”

We were in the kitchen of my new home. Boxes were piled everywhere and I was overwhelmed.

“I don’t know. I mean, just get on a plane and come to the lake? I don’t know if this is gonna work. Look at this house! I have soooo much to do. I just don’t know.”

“I’d love for you to come to the lake and relax. It’ll be fun. No offense, but it looks like you could use some TLC. We don’t have to worry now about where this is going. We can just take it one step at a time. Besides, these boxes aren't going anywhere. Would it be so bad to take a break?"

Malcolm's eyes pleaded with me to take an insane leap, at a time when I thought I needed to plant myself firmly in my new life. I needed to experience "normal" again. Flying 600 miles to be with a man I didn't know well wasn't "normal." Returning the intensity of his gaze, I knew I trusted him.

"Okay—this is crazy! This is really crazy—but I'll do it."

Flying

Within a couple of days there was an envelope from Malcolm with my airline ticket and a surprise gift certificate from Mina's Spa in Chapel Hill. I called him, bursting with gratitude.

"You are very welcome. Mindy helped me figure out where to get the certificate. I was just thinking that you were working so hard taking care of your babies, and trying to unpack, maybe a massage would feel good right now."

"Feel good? I might never leave once I get on that table!"

Imagining that someone besides me was thinking about what I might want and need floored me. I couldn't remember the last time I had felt so spoiled. I was giddy with excitement.

The next weekend, I flew to Birmingham. The entire week before leaving I felt jumpy. Sitting on the airplane an unanticipated wave of sadness hit when I thought, "I am no longer Van's wife." Suddenly, I was ambiguous about my decision to make this journey. Tears spilled out of my eyes and I turned toward the window, hoping my neighbor wouldn't notice. By the time the plane reached Birmingham I had collected myself, but remained apprehensive. We talked and held hands during the one-hour ride to his home. Once I looked over at him while he was driving and thought, "Who is this guy really? Have you gone too far this time, Mary?"

I looked out the car window into the pitch-black night. After forty minutes of driving, we exited the highway, making lots of twists and turns on dark, rural roads. Every once in a while the headlights illuminated horses and cows grazing in pastures. Finally we pulled into his long, gravel driveway and Malcolm parked the car in the garage. He popped out of the car and opened the door to the house, switching on the lights in the kitchen. The fresh smells of wood and new home greeted us. I had prepared myself for a not-so-clean or well-decorated bachelor pad. However, when I entered Malcolm's home, I knew this was a man who cared about his sense of place.

Off of the kitchen was a large great room shaped like a modified octagon. I quietly walked around and took notice of the surroundings of this man who had swiftly taken up residence in my heart. The high ceilings, abundant windows, romantic candles, and unusual multi-colored brick fireplace that went all the way to the ceiling told me much about Malcolm.

"This is gorgeous!" I beamed. Malcolm released an audible sigh of relief.

"Thank you. I love it here, but it's more fun to share it than to be here alone. Would you like to walk out onto the deck?"

Cold air enveloped us as we moved to the edge of the deck and leaned against the railing. Other than the trickle of a small waterfall off to our right and the sound of water meeting rocks below, the night was soothingly still. Country smells filled the air.

"Look up," Malcolm said.

"Oh my God! I haven't seen this many stars since living in Yellowstone! This is amazing. I can see why you love it here. It's so peaceful." Malcolm had been standing next to me. He stepped behind me and wrapped his arms around my waist. We stood in silence gazing at the lights hanging from the night sky.

In the morning, light streamed into the great room and it felt like we were perched in a tree house on a high rock bluff overlooking the lake. The expansive view was all water and trees.

"Would you like a latte?" Malcolm asked.

"You have a latte maker?"

"Well, when I saw that you loved them last week, I went out and bought a latte machine and big mugs," he said sheepishly.

At first I thought, *how considerate*. And then a wave of concern washed over me. What if the latte maker lasts longer than I do? Something about having anyone making decisions with me in mind set off internal alarms.

As the weekend progressed we slowly relaxed into a comfortable rhythm together. We spent the weekend taking long walks in the cold, baring secrets, cooking romantic meals, and drinking wine in front of the fireplace.

Late Sunday afternoon, I packed up my belongings and Malcolm put my suitcase in the trunk of the car. Driving in a car seemed jarring and offensive compared to the romantic solitude of the weekend. We decided to eat at a Mexican restaurant near the airport before my flight. Dipping my chip in the salsa, I looked across the table at this man who had seemed like a near stranger just ten days before. Tears welled up in my eyes, streaming black mascara tracks across my cheeks.

"I am so sad to leave you," I cried.

Malcolm reached across the table and grabbed my hands.

"Oh baby, sweet Mary Bea. I hate to see you go. We'll figure this out. It's gonna be okay. I promise. I don't know how things will work out. But it's gonna be okay." He took his napkin and wiped my tears away. I felt foolish. How could this attraction be so strong already? And how did he know that calling me "Mary Bea" would sound like a love song to me?

A week later, we were talking on the phone before going to sleep, a habit we had fast developed. Malcolm was in Alabama and I was in North Carolina.

"Baby, I'm gonna do it different this time. I'm going to stay open hearted and completely honest with you," Malcolm said, "no matter what."

Fear pierced me. Whoa! If he was going to be open hearted and honest, that meant I would have to be too. I had never done that before. Even though I was hesitant, I committed to do the same. Within days I shocked myself by blurting out, “This feels like falling in love.”

Long-Distance Love

For the next fifteen months we spent nearly all of my kid-free weekends together. Either I would fly to his secluded lake home or he would come to Chapel Hill and we would go out with friends. We were intoxicated with each other. Each morning when we were apart we would commute together via cell phone. I would call him after I dropped the kids off at school while he was traveling the hour into Birmingham. Like giddy teenagers, we ended our days on the phone, lying in bed laughing, sometimes crying, yet always sharing our days. The moments in between were filled with emails, calls, and text messages. Logic told me this was too much, too soon. My head tried to cry “Stop!” numerous times, but my heart ignored it.

Friends and family were happy for me, and understandably concerned at the speed we were moving. When I asked one close friend whose advice I valued, “What do you think about this thing with Malcolm?” her reply was frank.

“Right guy, wrong time,” she said.

I remember being advised, “Yes, the first post-divorce relationship can be very intense.”

I almost panicked the first time Malcolm pulled out his palm pilot and started marking off which weekends he would come to North Carolina and which ones I would come to Alabama. I wanted to slow down the process and reach back for my fledgling independence. Yet when we chose to miss a weekend, I ached to be in his arms.

Running

Before we started dating, I had decided to train for the San Diego Marathon. Never having run a marathon before, it was one of the big things I wanted to check off before I died. After a few weeks, Malcolm announced that he was training for the marathon too. Although he had been an athlete in college, distance running was not his favorite sport.

"I figure if I want to see you at all on the weekends, I'm gonna need to be running beside you," Malcolm kidded.

We printed out identical training schedules. When we were apart, he would run the same distance in Alabama, or wherever he was traveling for work, as I ran in North Carolina, or wherever I was traveling for work. We would encourage each other and check in over the phone. Most of the long runs were on the weekends and so every weekend we were together would include two or three long runs.

A couple of months into our training, we were on one of our longer runs, feet hitting the pavement in rhythm. Malcolm smiled at me.

"You know, this training for a marathon is great preparation for life for us," he said. "It isn't a sprint, and some days it's easier to run than others." I wasn't sure what he was trying to say. "Sometimes the weather is great, sometimes it's pretty bad. But this can be great preparation for our life together if you think about it—like a marathon."

There needs to be a word for that paradoxical sensation which describes the simultaneous experience of euphoria and fear, maybe *fearaphoria*. That's what I felt for the next ten miles, fearaphoria.

Milkshakes

I wasn't sure how to introduce Brendan and Kiki to Malcolm. They knew I was spending a lot of time with this man when they were at their Dad's, and they heard me on the phone in the evening. When

Malcolm and I talked about the best way to proceed with the kids, he was very clear.

"We need to let them dictate the pace. I've been down this road before and I think it's really important for Brendan and Kiki to be ready. This is all pretty new for them."

Taking my cue from Malcolm, who had experienced his own father dating after the death of his mother and had deeply loved the son of his previous girlfriend, I waited until the children brought up the subject of meeting him. One day when I was scratching Brendan's back before he went to sleep, he turned his head to the side and looked up at me.

"Mom, can I meet Malcolm?"

"Sure, honey. I bet we can figure something out next time he's in town."

Malcolm and I decided it would be best to keep the first meeting brief and to pick Brendan up from a friend's house instead of Van's. I offered for Kiki to join us, but she wasn't interested. Brendan jumped into the back seat of the car. The short drive to the Loop, a burger and pizza joint, was uneventful. At the restaurant I sat next to Brendan, Malcolm across from us. The guys hit it off immediately. Malcolm waited for Brendan to ask him questions. Sipping his Oreo milkshake, Brendan grilled Malcolm.

"What is your favorite car?"

"I drive an older Volvo, but I guess I would say Maserati if money didn't matter," Malcolm answered.

"What kind of boat do you have? What size is the engine? How much horsepower? In-board or out?"

Like most pre-teen boys, Brendan loved technology. When he saw Malcolm had a trendy phone, he was impressed. It was a huge step to share Brendan with Malcolm. I was glad their first meeting went well.

The more honest I was with Malcolm about my true feelings, the more he responded in kind. We each risked baring the dark parts of our souls and our worst mistakes. I learned to listen in a new way. Afraid that this gentle man would be offended by my fiery outbursts with Brendan and Kiki, I implored, “If you *really* knew what it was like in this house, you would head for the hills.”

He assured me he wasn’t worried. Slowly we let him in to the insanity of our family life; most of the time it went well.

“You may want to date other men so you have no regrets later,” Malcolm offered on more than one occasion. I thought about it, but I already couldn’t imagine not being with Malcolm. At times my unresolved anger with Van created a wedge between Malcolm and me. One time I asked Malcolm for a little space so I could clarify which of my disturbing feelings were old and which were new. Also, I wanted to be sure that I was holding on to “me” while we were becoming “we.” Eyes moist with emotion, he assured me, “Take all the time you need. I’ll be waiting.”

It didn’t take much time.

With speed and surety that defied sanity, our lives, our hearts, and our souls fused. In his arms I felt both protected and set free. It was in Malcolm’s arms that I came home. The meaning of the last line of the mysterious poem I had written months ago—the day before we first kissed, was beginning to make sense: “Pastor, mentor, lover…come home, come home.”

Part Six: Searching

"However men try to reach me,
I return their love with my love;
Whatever path they may travel,
It leads to me in the end. "
—From the *Bhagavad Gita*

Let Jesus in the Boat?

Malcolm pulled the car into a parking space far away from the entrance to the United Church of Chapel Hill. The spot was the closest one available. We held hands walking through the parking lot. I read the bumper stickers along the way, "Peace is patriotic," and "To believe is to care, to care is to do." After years of meeting interesting people who belonged to this church, I finally decided to visit.

The sunlit sanctuary was contemporary, yet the pews and the massive, glowing, light-colored wood cross added warmth. Seating was theater style; each row was slightly higher than the one before. Most inviting was the large bank of clear windows overlooking woods and a walking path.

Listening to the pianist while waiting for the service to begin, I felt comfortable. Seated around us in the pews were people whose diversity reflected the Chapel Hill community. There were men in tweeds and women in flowing "earth mother" skirts or Doncaster suits. Some teen girls were in dresses, others in baggy jeans. I noticed that if we attended here, Brendan and Kiki could worship in a place where traditional families joined families with two moms, step-moms, or no moms. Yin and yang were interwoven in co-pastors Richard and Jill Edens. Since Malcolm had been a United Church of Christ minister in Connecticut, this style of worship was familiar for him.

It had been nearly two years since Lama Norlha said, "You were raised a Christian; perhaps it is time you should go home," and I still hadn't found a spiritual community. Even though Divine

Presence had always been a part of my world, my awareness of it expanded in this new life. I was confident of the connection, but still felt frustratingly confused about how to define the relationship.

We continued to visit UCCH whenever we were in Chapel Hill. After a few visits alone and some with Malcolm, I decided to include Brendan and Kiki. At first they resisted. They were normal pre-teens and we had been out of the church routine for a few years. Each week there were more familiar faces to greet me, but I wanted to take time before joining.

On a rare kid-free, Malcolm-less Sunday, I slipped into a pew halfway down the sanctuary. Leaning against the hard, unforgiving wood, a wave of exhaustion moved through my body. Absently, I touched my right hand to my left breast, acknowledging a dull pain in my heart.

Staring at the cross hanging behind the altar, I wondered whether I had over-extended myself again. Contrary to my initial understanding, I was now required to travel frequently for my job. Between travel for work and romance, my green suitcase constantly remained in my bedroom on "high alert." My cell phone bills were so high that Verizon could have named a tower in my honor. When I was in North Carolina I would spend hours on the phone with Malcolm in Alabama. When I was in Alabama, I would call home to catch up with Brendan and Kiki. When I was traveling for work, I called them all. I was leaving fragments of myself all over the Southeast, pieces of broken glass.

Tilting my head back, I felt the warmth from the sun wash over me as clouds gave way outside and the sun broke free, extending her fingers through the sanctuary's long, rectangular windows. As the light danced around the church, waving her wand of illumination pew by pew, I reflected on recent disturbing conversations with my boss. I had allowed myself to be intimidated and the stress was taking its toll. My stomach was constantly in knots—literally. The pain was so great I was scheduled for a colonoscopy and endoscopy the next week. Worst of all, I no longer trusted my boss or believed the company could succeed under his leadership. I was being asked to say and do things that felt dishonest, yet I was afraid to speak my mind. Staring out the window, I wondered, how am I going to keep paying my bills, caring for my family, and maintain my integrity at the same time?

An audible sigh escaped from my lips as I turned my thoughts from work to Kiki. She still seemed unhappy in our new home. I was concerned that she was spiraling into a dark, sad place. Overwhelmed, my mind was racing with these disturbing thoughts. I sat in the pew visibly agitated, fidgeting with my skirt and the bulletin, crossing and uncrossing my legs. Eventually I settled in and looked up at the front of the church and listened to the young woman reading scripture.

> *When evening came, his disciples went down to the sea, got into a boat, and started across the sea to Capernaum. It was now dark, and Jesus had not yet come to them. The sea became rough because a strong wind was blowing. When they had rowed about three or four miles, they saw Jesus walking on the sea and coming near the boat, and they were terrified. But he said to them, "It is I; do not be afraid." Then they wanted to take him into the boat, and immediately the boat reached the land toward which they were going.*
> —John 6:16–21 NRSV Bible

I had heard this passage many times before. This time, I felt out of control and afraid. Unable to maintain my normal level of decorum, I began to sob. The young woman read the second reading.

> *For this reason I bow my knees before the Father, from whom every family in heaven and on earth*

> *takes its name. I pray that, according to the riches of his glory, he may grant that you may be strengthened in your inner being with power through his Spirit, and that Christ may dwell in your hearts through faith, as you are being rooted and grounded in love.*
> —Ephesians 3:14–17

I tried to stifle my sobs so that I wouldn't disturb the other worshippers—people I barely knew. I cast my eyes downward hoping that no one would see the unceasing flow of tears.

> *I pray that you may have the power to comprehend, with all the saints, what is the breadth and length and height and depth, and to know the love of Christ that surpasses knowledge, so that you may be filled with all the fullness of God.*
> —Ephesians 3:18–19

I could not for the life of me figure out what had hit me so hard. Tasting the salt of my unnamed grief, I felt an unbearably powerful desire to leave. I fumbled in my purse and found a tissue to blow my nose. The reading continued.

> *Now to him who by the power at work within us is able to accomplish abundantly far more than all we can ask or imagine, to him be glory in the church and in Christ Jesus to all generations, forever and ever. Amen.*
> —Ephesians 3:20–21

Although every muscle in my body twitched as if ready dash out of the church, I stayed. I was being pulled, as if by an invisible magnet, down into the pew. I stayed because the part of me that is stronger than my impulses, wiser than my thoughts, wouldn't let me leave. I knew there was more. I knew I needed to hear Richard's sermon.

Wiping my eyes and nose with a tissue and exhaling deeply, I watched Richard step to the podium and place his notes on the lectern. Richard looked boyish at fifty years old. Speaking with the distinctive accent of his North Carolina roots, Richard's commanding voice and message unleashed a new wave of emotions. Weary, yet alert, I listened as his words called forth even more tears. My vision blurred, I grabbed a pencil from the pew and began to write notes on the cream-colored bulletin. I scribbled the lines that most impacted me from Richard's sermon.

"Embracing unwanted change is one of life's greatest challenges."

"You can welcome Jesus into the boat."

"At the point of succumbing to our darkest fears, the dawn breaks."

And the one that pulled at me the most, "Do we trust that we will gain our lives in losing our lives?"

Shit! There was that trust thing again! Hadn't I trusted enough? Hadn't I changed enough? What could there possibly be left for me to lose? Was this primal reaction to the scripture and Richard's words an indicator that there was more to come? Was my unconscious response a "knowing" that it was time for me to take yet another look at my priorities, my lifestyle, and my faith? As if there was a boa constrictor in my gut, the knots of "knowing" tightened in my stomach—I wasn't done losing. There was something else I needed to let go of.

During communion, healing prayer was offered by Jill and the parish nurse, Aly. Desperate for help, I mustered the courage to walk over to the baptismal font and approach Jill and Aly. I looked into Jill's eyes, mascara smeared on my face.

"I would like for us to pray for healing for me and my daughter, Kiki. My stomach's in such pain I'm going to UNC for tests. My prayer for me is for clarity about the source of this pain and for healing. For Kiki, emotional healing." I stopped a moment, trying to collect myself. "She's so sad since my divorce and unhappy in our new home. I'm worried about her. I just wish I knew what I could do to help her."

Jill and Aly nodded their heads and Jill read from a small prayer book. The two women and I formed a human circle, with our arms locked around each other. Tears flowing, I allowed my fellow mothers to encircle me with their prayers. I felt safe with these women I didn't know, relieved to have finally called for help.

The next day I wrote in my journal, "What moved me so deeply? Words cheapen the experience…hard to explain. I believe there was some gift of grace that I don't completely understand. It's like I want to approach my faith in a whole new light. Thank you, God, for this gift, even though I don't quite understand it."

I continued later in my journal. "When Richard spoke of unwanted change, I thought of Kiki and how she has struggled with the change from the neighborhood that she loved to this new one. If I let Jesus into my boat, won't that help the kids let him into theirs? I'll bet there is a way I can follow this path and honor and incorporate other traditions. Why has it been so hard for me to commit to a way? To this way? Christ is a coming home for me. But can I really let Jesus in the boat?"

Staring out the window, I watched a squirrel devouring sunflower seeds from the bird feeder. Normally, I would send Daisy out to chase the squirrel away. Resigned to the intruder, I continued to write.

"If I let Jesus in, I need to know that everyone is welcome on this boat. Would Jesus throw Buddha, Mohammed, or a gay man overboard? My guess is he would catch some fish, give thanks for it, and eat it with them—the same way he ate with Gentiles, sinners, and tax collectors. I'll bet he would engage in respectful, serious debate; the same way he debated with the priests in the temple. Imagine Jesus, Buddha, Krishna, and Mohammed drifting in a boat off of the Sea of Capernaum. I'll bet they would find they had much in common. I'll bet they would agree to disagree respectfully. I would love to be rowing that boat.

"If I finally let Jesus in my boat, wouldn't I be following Lama Norlha's advice to *choose* a path and follow it devoutly, wholeheartedly? I can't deny the power of my experience yesterday. Couldn't I create a Christian path that embraced the Divine Feminine? One that welcomed all to the table? One that honored social activism? Are the stirrings in my heart really contrary to the teachings of Christ? Or are they contrary to the doctrines of true Christian teaching? This new path will require courage."

I stopped writing and simply sat cross-legged on the carpet in my bedroom and reread one of the passages in the Tao Te Ching that I had read years before on Mt. Diablo, "Do you have the patience to wait till your mud settles and the water is clear? Can you remain unmoving till the right action arises by itself?"

The mud in my soul was so stirred up that it would take a lot of waiting for me to experience clarity. I leaned against the foot of my bed, the mattress pressing into my back, and resumed my writing. "I feel so weary. I'm willing to surrender this desire for a less busy life to God, Spirit—whatever your name is. You know who you are. I'm not doing such a great job on my own; I'm ready to hand it over to you. I trust and know that there are possibilities that I cannot imagine."

I took a few deep breaths and put my journal and pen on the floor next to me. Slowly, I leaned back and lowered myself into the yoga pose for surrender, *sirvasana.* Sprawled out spread-eagle on my back, I closed my eyes and breathed deeply, remembering the words of a former yoga teacher, "breathing in love and support… breathing out fear and pain…breathing in love and support… breathing out fear and pain…."

Melting into the carpet, gradually the tension released from my head, neck, back, arms, legs, and feet. "Breathing in love and support…breathing out fear and pain….” My breaths deepened; a sense of calm washed over me. “Breathing in love and support… breathing out fear and pain…”

Over the next few days I moved differently. Sometimes I left dishes in the sink. Sometimes I didn't respond to emails right away. Sometimes I watched my cell phone ring incessantly like a ranting toddler, and didn't answer. Slowly, the mud began to settle.

When I expressed my emotional and somewhat confusing reaction to the “Let Jesus in the Boat” sermon to a good friend, she recommended that I read Marcus Borg's book, *Meeting Jesus Again for the First Time*.

“That might be a Jesus you could let in your boat,” she intimated.

She was right. Borg introduced me to a Jesus I wanted to learn from, maybe even follow.—not a condemning, judging Jesus, but a radical, compassionate, social justice Jesus. Borg was the switch that turned on a light inside of me. I wanted to learn more about my Christian roots. Surprisingly I found Jesus as interesting and insightful as I had found Buddha and Lao-Tzu—only with one great difference. The stories of Jesus were the stories of my growing up, the stories of my family. Borg's perspective on Jesus helped me see that the Christian I wanted to be was not only alright, but actually closely aligned with the raw teachings of Jesus.

Certain passages in Borg's book were so different from anything I had read before that I had to return to them over and over again. I wanted to follow “the way that leads to life” that Borg described.

“The narrow way, the way less traveled is the alternative wisdom of Jesus. It has two closely related dimensions. First it is an invitation to see God as gracious and womblike rather than as the source and enforcer of the requirements, boundaries, and divisions of conventional wisdom. Second, it is an invitation to a path that leads away from the life of conventional wisdom to a life that is more and more centered in God."

Remembering and Forgetting

Although my emotional experience at church compelled me to move at a more measured pace, I was still busy working and taking care of Brendan and Kiki. My office was in the bonus room, directly above my bedroom. Occasionally I would be woken up at 5:00 a.m. by the fax machine churning out documents and rattling the floor above me. I felt so invaded!

For too long I thought I was powerless against these invasions. I believed that if I didn't respond immediately, even on the weekends, my job would be on the line. I worried about what others would think of me if I only worked Monday–Friday, nine to five. So I chose to change that. On Friday, I left my office, shut the door and vowed not to return until Monday morning. What an enlightening experiment! It was *hard* not to go up and check my email, fax machine, and business line. As much as I whined and moaned about the demands placed on me, I realized I had begun to define myself by others' need of me. I was addicted to checking email. I actually had to stop myself from going upstairs at least ten times that first Saturday.

In a weird way, I envied our dogs, Boomer and Daisy. When I put them in the backyard, our fence decided for them where they could or couldn't go—a clear dividing line between our property and the neighbors'. Creating a separation between work and home wasn't as simple for me. But choosing to find the right balance between the two proved to be a good first step. Slowly I found myself "being" a little more, and "doing" a little less.

Anne Morrow Lindbergh wrote, "For it is only framed in space that beauty blooms." Inspired by her wisdom, I reinstituted my morning ritual of beginning my days with an inspirational activity that would fuel my soul, such as reading, journaling, yoga, or meditation. Each morning I would rise before the sun and make space for me. The extra clarity was worth the sleep loss. Honoring my need to be grounded, I took walks in the woods as often as possible. My time outdoors reminded me of the primal call of my own nature; the same primal call that coaxed primitive woman to dance naked under the moon. I chose to sit in the lap of the Creator each day, not for the sake of the Creator, but to allow space for the Creator within me to fuse with the Creator of all. From that space came moments of inspiration—inspiration that felt like a song singing me back to me. From the silence came new ideas that had room to breathe. In the past, they had been choked by faxes, emails, and phone calls.

How had I allowed myself to be knocked off-center by overcommitment again? I was a living example of Rabbi Rami Shapiro's words, "Remembering and forgetting is my spiritual journey." Once again, I was ready to come clean about my life choices—ugh! Hadn't I been down this road before? The starting point was my job. I felt an inexplicable freedom when I finally declared to myself, "The money's great, the travel sucks, and the lies are killing me!"

At first, I had no idea what I would do with that truth, but just acknowledging it allowed me to face my choices honestly. Moving the stone that had been covering this truth allowed me to peer beneath the rock and see the belief system that had helped get me into this mess. I had bought into an erroneous idea that joyful employment and financial freedom were mutually exclusive. I wanted to let that belief out in the open so that it could die under the blazing sun of truth.

Taking time to read and complete the exercises in Wayne Muller's *How, Then, Shall We Live?* and Martha Beck's *Finding Your Own North Star* helped me to dream up a crazy new venture. When I wasn't sure how to define this venture, I called my good friend Peter.

"I want to create a place where people can dream and scheme and I can support them in making those dreams come true," I said. "I want to take what I have learned and shift from care of the dying to care of the living."

I paused to let my speeding heart slow a notch, "But who pays for that? What do you call that?"

"Mary, that's what I do," Peter laughed. "It's called life coaching—and people do pay for it. I love it! In a way, you do it very naturally already."

That conversation planted the seed for my next venture, LifeDesign Studio. I drew on my financial planning skills to create a bare-bones budget for my family. The deprivation I occasionally felt in denying myself *any* unnecessary purchases was offset by the sense of freedom I experienced as I began saving money during the next six months so I could quit my job. I began pushing back occasionally when my boss asked me to travel. During those six months, the racing engine that was my life began to slow down. When I realized I didn't have to be a slave to my job, I felt a new sense of empowerment. When I took time to be still and slowed the pace of life, I felt as if I were watching the fog that shrouded me lift. I knew I needed to pull back in other areas, as well. One evening during my nightly telephone ritual with Malcolm, I broached a difficult subject.

"I need to slow down even more than I have because I want to be more present with Brendan and Kiki. Also, I need to time to get clear about what I'm going to do with my life. I think I'm going to need to come to the lake less often."

I paused and waited for a response, but there was none.

"I still want to see you as much—more, really. I wish we could be together more often and I could stay home. I just don't see how that can happen."

"I'm not surprised," Malcolm finally said. "You've got a lot going on and I've already been thinking, maybe there is a way that I can come and stay longer in Chapel Hill." I was relieved he wasn't hurt. "I can look into working from Chapel Hill one week out of every month. It's easier for me to come there than it is for you to come here and I'm willing to give this a try," he finished.

I felt like I was drinking in his deep, melodic, southern drawl.

"Thank you."

Melding Yankee Catholic and Southern Baptist

The bond with Malcolm was moving from a whirlwind, swept-off-my-feet experience to a deep, passionate love. If this love were to be given a chance to grow, I needed to weed out my small, convenient deceptions. Even though we had discussed our diverse backgrounds, there were times when I would hide pieces of my true spiritual experiences and beliefs because I was afraid they would be too radical for Malcolm. I was afraid if he knew what I really believed he would not want to be in relationship with me. As Malcolm and I spent more time together, our discussions around faith deepened. He seemed so secure in his beliefs; I found that threatening. His confidence magnified my confusion. Our upbringings were as different as if we were raised on separate planets.

Malcolm's family didn't own playing cards when he was growing up because they associated cards with gambling. My parents frequently invited neighbors over to fire up their Irish coffee maker. It was difficult for me to fall asleep on those evenings when the boisterous crowd downstairs would "ooohhh" and "aaahhhh" as Dad ignited the Irish whiskey.

Afraid to lose myself again to someone else's agenda, I demanded, and Malcolm respected, my need for lots of space to explore my personal relationship with the Sacred. Whenever I sensed any input from him that might be leading me down the traditional Christian path, I felt my body tense.

***

One morning when we were driving to Clemson for a football game, our discussion took a theological turn. I felt defensive and went on the attack.

"Well, I can't stand when churches get all worked up about the 'sin' and 'saving' stuff and forget about the lessons Jesus taught," I said. "You know, those unimportant little things like forgiveness, compassion and loving your neighbor." Turning to him defiantly, I said, trembling, "If you're waiting for some magic moment when I declare that Jesus Christ is my Lord and Savior so that you can 'save' me, you need to know that is not going to happen."

"Hey, baby, that's fine. I'm not expecting anything from you. I was just saying what I believe."

Stung, Malcolm looked straight ahead, gripping the steering wheel.

Leaning my back against the passenger door, I gazed at Malcolm and felt regret for overreacting.

"I'm sorry. I don't know why I feel so defensive about this." I paused to gather my thoughts. "It's just that I don't want to pretend to be something I'm not. And I don't want you to feel like you need to do that either. I love going to your church when we are in Birmingham because Sarah is a gifted preacher and the people are nice to me. But this whole Baptist thing is really hard."

"I understand that." Malcolm said. "I struggle with it too. I just want you to understand, not all Baptists are conservative Southern Baptists. I mean, we have a vibrant gay community and a woman as a pastor. It's not like I'm coming from the Dark Ages."

"I just want to make sure you understand that by going, I'm not saying I agree with everything that even a moderate Baptist church espouses."

"I hear you. And by the way, I don't either."

"It's not just a Baptist thing," I torturously grasped for words that would clarify how I felt—for both of us. "I've been to so many different churches; I don't think there is a denomination that fits for me. I'm settled on 'child of God.' And by the way, the God I praise is bigger than words like He or She."

"That's fine. I don't know what you want me to say."

I didn't know either.

***

Occasionally when I mentioned my beliefs about past lives, tarot, or other non-traditional spiritual concepts, Malcolm would make a skeptical remark. I wasn't sure how to interpret his body language when these subjects came up. I sensed he felt uncomfortable and it looked to me like he wanted to say, "Do you really believe that stuff?" Because I was unsure of myself, I would shut down and withhold my feelings when I thought we were approaching a topic we might not agree on. I knew the consequences of withholding information too well. If I wanted this love to grow in a healthy way, I'd have to risk honesty.

At times, the subtle language around Malcolm's genteel, southern upbringing was confusing to this northern girl; just as my swearing and wild experiences were foreign to him. If we were going to grow together as a couple, it was time to communicate openly about our diverse pasts and how they might impact our future.

On one of his visits, we sat on the porch swing at my house; encircled by the beautiful colors of fall. I turned to face Malcolm, "I know you don't think that tarot readings are real. But I have to tell you, my experiences with tarot, both with Becky and Rhonda, have been powerful. I'm not asking you to believe what I believe, but I'm not willing to deny my beliefs or 'tone down' who I am in any way to be in this relationship. This isn't just about tarot readings; do you understand what I'm trying to say?"

"I think so," Malcolm said. We sat in tense silence for a few moments.

"I'm sorry, Mary Bea," he said. "I think sometimes when I hear things that are so foreign to me I unconsciously react negatively to them."

"Well, I'm finding myself anticipating that and closing off parts of myself to you. I don't want to do that. I want to keep my promise to you to stay open-hearted."

He looked at me thoughtfully, brushed my hair out of my face, put his arm around me and pulled me close to him. Kissing the top of my head, he said, "Baby, you are living your faith. I'm learning so much from you just watching the way you are devoted to your practices. I fell in love with you just the way you are and don't want you to change one bit. Not one little bit."

He held me tight and said, "I'd be lying if I didn't say some of what you believe is different than what I believe. But I don't think just because we love each other we have to agree on everything. I think we're close enough on the big stuff."

I moved in closer, putting my head on his shoulder.

"Thank you. I guess part of what I want us to agree on is to be respectful of each other's beliefs. I need to work on that one—I think I can be pretty judgmental of traditional Christianity," I said, thinking, *I must have been awfully good in a past life to deserve a love like this*.

African Treasures

Malcolm's shoulders were hunched forward, his feet were shuffling, and he desperately needed a shave. As soon as I saw him, I wanted to run past the Birmingham airport security gate and throw myself into his weary arms. When he was about fifteen yards away, he raised his head and noticed me. His gait quickened and I moved forward. We hungrily embraced. Three weeks apart was more than we had ever endured. Twenty-four hours after departing Lusaka, Zambia, Malcolm had the marks of one who had traveled through many time zones—dark circles under his eyes and rumpled clothing.

The next morning, we hunkered down on the sofa, wrapped in quilts made by Miss White, one of those sort-of relatives that people seem to have in the South. Having never met Miss White,

I only had family lore to go by. She was a prolific quilter who continued to sew well into her nineties. When she found out that Malcolm had built a home on the lake, she invited him to come over and pick out some quilts. The day he arrived with his stepmother, Jimmie Ruth, Miss White opened a closet that was stacked with at least twenty-five quilts and offered for him to take as many as he wanted.

Now Miss White's quilts held us as we sipped cups of coffee, surrounded by birds twittering at the feeder and trees bravely urging their new buds out into the world. Suspended in this tree-house-like setting, with hours to talk undisturbed, Malcolm was unsure where to begin, or how to describe his three-week trip to Southern Africa. He decided to read his journal passages out loud. I was mesmerized as he read one moving story after another. He occasionally grabbed his digital camera to find a picture of the person he was talking about.

"This is a mother holding her dying baby in the hospital," he said, voice cracking with emotion. "They don't have enough nurses, none really, and so the mothers come and serve as nurses for the babies in the hospital. They sleep on the floor with their babies because there aren't enough beds either." A distant look washed over his face, tears welling in his eyes.

"This is Mike, one of the boys at the orphanage. I think he's about eight. He really got to me. When the nuns asked me to give a blessing, he prayed instead—one of the most fervent prayers I've ever heard. I didn't understand a word of it because he spoke in his tribal tongue, but listening to him made me cry."

Malcolm cried again as he talked about Mike. I wanted to fly to Zambia and adopt the little boy with the bulging brown eyes and green stuff coming out of his nose.

"Here's the wife of the president of the University of Botswana. She's quite a scholar. Talking to her helped me understand the role that discrimination against women, lack of education, and inability to own property plays in the spread of

HIV/AIDS in Africa."

For hours Malcolm continued to read from his journal, expand on the stories, and show pictures. Any one of his experiences would have been life-changing. After three weeks of continuous exposure to tragedy and courage, fear and hope, poverty and gratitude, the flame in Malcolm that was called to "create connection and community for people when they need it most" was blazing.

"Look at this little video. I had so much fun! You're gonna laugh. This is in Cape Town at the Nelson Mandela Square near the Apartheid Museum. Paul filmed this for me when were at the celebration for ten years of democratic government in South Africa."

I watched the small screen on the camera as a light-hearted, baseball-capped Malcolm, the only white person in the video, danced to the music of the Soweto Gospel Choir. He was right; I laughed—how could I not, seeing him move with such unencumbered joy?

"That museum was like nothing I've ever seen before. It reminded me of what happened here with the Civil Rights movement."

Anyone who has given birth knows words cannot convey that transformative experience. Listening to Malcolm try to explain the magnitude of his African encounters reminded me of my post-birthing attempts to explain the inexplicable. I felt love and admiration for his caring-explorer spirit. I stared out the window, watching the goldfinches that were turning more yellow each day vigorously attack thistle seeds in the feeder. Emotionally raw from the magnitude of suffering and stigma he had witnessed, Malcolm's tears were never far from the surface. When he reached his journal entry on April 18, he smiled and read,

"Mary Bea, one thing this trip has taught me is I don't want to be away from you for long periods of time anymore.... *I want to marry you.*" Malcolm moved closer, no longer reading from his journal.

"Whenever the time is right, I'm ready," he said. "I'm done. Life is short. I don't need to wait any longer to know what I want. I don't know how we're gonna work this thing out with you in Chapel Hill and me here. I think we need to decide what's most important and let everything else fall in place behind that."

He leaned over and kissed me passionately. "For me, what's most important is that you, Brendan, Kiki, and I become a family. Whatever that looks like."

Laughing and crying I wrapped my arms around his waist as he pulled me closer to him. This wasn't the first time we had talked about marriage, but this time we weren't talking about "sometime," we were talking about "soon."

Surprisingly, I had no doubt it was right for us to move ahead. Later I looked in my own journal and marveled that on the same day Malcolm wrote about wanting to get married, thousands of miles away I had penned, "Yesterday I cleaned every closet. My closets have room for Malcolm now. My heart has room for Malcolm. My life has room for Malcolm."

Interdependence Day

Forgoing the expense and busyness of a planned ceremony in September, we eloped at the Birmingham Botanical Gardens on July 4, our self-proclaimed "Interdependence Day." Brendan and Kiki were an integral part of the planning and the ceremony. Excitement coursed through the house as we chose the readings, wrote the vows, bought the rings and clothes, and arranged the honeymoon, all within five days. Kiki and Brendan repeatedly referred to the ceremony as "our wedding."

We pledged to tell only our Birmingham minister, Sarah, and our friend Judy. Brendan offered to dye his hair brown again since he knew I wasn't excited about the blonde 'do he had adopted a couple of months before. The blonde was growing out and he was a tiger-striped brown and blonde. Thankful that he wasn't green (as he had been just before the blonde), I responded, "No, this is real. This way we'll never forget your fourteen-year-old hair-experimenting phase."

Kiki and I dressed at Judy's home before the wedding. In her oversized bathroom, we took turns showering and blowing each other's hair dry, using the bride and bridesmaid baskets of toiletries Judy has thoughtfully placed there for us. When we were done, Judy painted Kiki's nails on the patio.

On our way to the Botanical Gardens, Judy couldn't contain her excitement and belted out, "Going to the chapel and we're gonna get maaaaarried…." Kiki and I chimed in laughing. At the gardens my mood shifted from giddy to pensive. The sun was almost directly overhead, the sky a celestial blue—the same color as Kiki's satin halter dress. Kiki and I floated up the long sidewalk together. I felt conspicuous in my white, sequined gown until I saw Malcolm, Brendan, and Sarah's glowing smiles. My eyes locked on Malcolm and my body automatically moved toward him. I was struck by the gravity of the moment, but wasn't afraid.

Sarah and the four of us formed a circle under the Gazebo in the Rose Garden. Stillness and the beauty of simple ritual blanketed us. Occasionally we would be reminded there was a world beyond us when we heard the click of Judy's camera, or the wind carrying the smell of roses.

Sarah asked Kiki to hold my bouquet of white roses so that I could turn and face Malcolm. When my heart started beating again I found the hands I had admired at our first dinner together firmly holding mine. I saw those liquid blue eyes drinking me up. I felt protective of that tender heart when I pledged, "I promise to love you with an open heart, to listen deeply to your innermost thoughts, and to be considerate and tender in my care of you. With God's help, I vow to continue to be your best friend, to encourage your spiritual growth, and to walk with you in times of joy and sorrow, as long as we both shall live. Amen."

I must have been breathing when Malcolm pledged the same to me, it just seemed as if all creation stopped. Sensitive to the importance of this ceremony for Brendan and Kiki, Sarah gave each of them an opportunity to speak. Brendan bowed his multi-colored head, raised his arms over us and led us in an eloquent, heart-felt blessing. When it was Kiki's turn, she bounced up and down in her high heel sandals squealing,

"I'm so happy! This is the right thing to do at the right time! I am so *happy*!"

***

After we were married, Malcolm started working from Chapel Hill three weeks out of every month. This meant that most of the time when the kids were with me, so was their new stepdad, or as Brendan called Malcolm, "my second dad." Kiki had to be more conscious of what she was or wasn't wearing around the house. Brendan occasionally pushed back at any feeling of being disciplined by Malcolm. Malcolm gave up working in the office he loved and living in the home of his dreams and took on driving 600 miles each way twice a month. Sometimes I felt torn between my loyalty for my new husband and my loyalty to my kids.

A few months into our new life, we decided to sit down and have a family meeting. There had been a few blow-ups and we wanted to relieve the tension. Each person was given an opportunity to express how they felt. Kiki glared at Malcolm.

"You don't need to protect my mom from me," she said. "I've been walking in on her in the bathroom my whole life."

Malcolm winced at the verbal blow, took a breath and responded. "Kiki, I'm sorry. It's hard for me to see anyone mistreat your mom. I'm new at this too. I've never done this before either."

Toward the end of the meeting we took time to say what we appreciated about each other. Kiki looked at Malcolm again and smiled. "You've brought order to this family. I like that we have a routine again."

On one hand, we were excited and enjoying the process of melding as a family. On the other, we were feeling the pressure physically and financially of maintaining two homes, starting a new business, forgoing alimony, and managing busy teenager schedules. Trying to coordinate Brendan and Kiki's time with their dad and Malcolm's time in Alabama, I felt like an air traffic controller.

One Saturday when Malcolm was at the lake with a friend, I spent the entire day in bed worried, overwhelmed, and exhausted. Guilt consumed me when Brendan asked if I would drive him and a friend to a skateboard park. Barely lifting my head off the pillow I mumbled that I just didn't have the energy. I lacked Malcolm's faith that "everything would work out." Tired of the fragmented family, I longed for all of us to be in one place all of the time. I couldn't see how we could do that with Malcolm's job, our primary source of income, located in Alabama, and my new business as well as Brendan and Kiki's life in North Carolina.

There were a few tense conversations over how to reduce the financial burdens we were bearing. The most obvious options were for us to sell the lake house or for me to leave my new business and get a "real" job. Both options felt like a poison pill. I never regretted getting married when we did, but I worried that I had taken on more than I could handle, yet again.

Emergency Room Insight

Like a couple of fish swimming along unaware of the shark behind us, Malcolm and I continued swimming through our bi-state life until the shark bit in the form of an emergency room visit. I was with a client when my cell phone kept ringing; I turned it off so it wouldn't bother us. When my office phone began to ring, I pulled the plug. Only when my client left did I realize Malcolm was desperately trying to reach me. I listened to one of his messages.

"I'm having pains in my chest, I'm going to drive to UNC Hospital and get it checked out. It's probably nothing; I'll call you when I know something." Thankfully, after two days of tests, it was determined that Malcolm was in great shape. A young cardiologist sauntered in to discharge Malcolm and tell us there was nothing wrong.

"I think this is totally stress-related," I said in a motherly tone.

Standing in his white coat and assured nature, the cardiologist, who looked barely old enough to drink beer, stared blankly at me as if I had just spoken to him in Swahili.
Malcolm, standing in his blue hospital gown, asked, "I'm supposed to fly out to Chicago and give a two-day training tomorrow. Will that be okay?" My jaw dropped.

"I see no reason why not," the doctor answered without missing a beat. "Your heart is sound; we checked everything thoroughly."

"Maybe if this is all stress-related it would be good for him to take a couple of days and rest?" I chimed in, more than a little flabbergasted. Trained only in the medical and not the emotional workings of the heart, this bright young man had, I thought, missed the diagnosis completely.

The next day, instead of boarding a plane, Malcolm helped me load Boomer and Daisy into the car for a walk in the woods. I had said my piece: "This back and forth to Alabama is going to kill you."

It had been a full year since we decided to get married and "figure it out later." Malcolm's body and my worrying was telling us that later was here. Like families who know it is time to call in hospice, we chose to look at options that felt like death.

We walked in silence for a while, listening to our feet falling on the soft dirt path.

"Let's just sell the lake house," Malcolm whispered, his voice tired and sounding weak, broken. "I'll figure out where to stay when I work in Birmingham, but at least we won't have two house payments. Probably I could find a job here eventually anyway."

His shoulders slouched and his face lined in grief, Malcolm stopped walking for a minute. We stood in the path holding each other until holding didn't help any longer. I tried to absorb the magnitude of Malcolm's offer. He was passionate about his work and the lake house. How could this plan work? It was April again, and the emerging buds were encouraging us to trust in new life, but our heavy hearts couldn't see what new life would look like for us. I knew the cost of giving up dreams. I didn't want either of us to have to make that choice.

A few days later we sat on the back porch with Brendan and Kiki to tell them of our decision. The sour smell of freshly-cut grass filled the air. Positioned around the table like four directionals on a weathervane, we were unaware of the way the wind was about to blow. Malcolm wanted to be the one to tell the kids about the lake house.

"Your mom and I have been talking and we think that even though everything is okay with me physically, we believe the trip to the ER was a wake up call. We need to look at doing some things differently."

Brendan squirmed in his chair, visibly uncomfortable with what might be coming. Both kids had heard hard and unexpected news before.

"We're going to sell the lake house."

There was silence for a few minutes and then Kiki leaned back in her chair the way moms hate for their children to do.

"Why do we have to sell the lake house? Why don't we sell this one and go to that prep school mom talked about?"

Wide-eyed, Malcolm and I stared at each other, and then at her.

"Are you serious?" I asked.

"Totally. Dad is in California with his girlfriend most of the time now and almost all of my friends will be going to East instead of Chapel Hill High. And I have never liked this house."

"Brendan, what do you think?" Malcolm asked.

"I'm not sure. I love the lake and the boat, but I'm not sure. I'm willing to think about it, though." I gripped the edge of the table as if that would stop my world from spinning.

Scouting Home

Three weeks later we flew to Alabama and toured St. Bernard Prep School. From the moment we left the airport in the rental car I scanned the scenery not with the eyes of a visitor, but with the eyes of a would-be resident. The trip to the house took an hour. I had driven this drive hundreds of times. Would it bug me to be so far from the city? Turning off the highway onto the county road, I noticed trash I had not seen before. Would I be embarrassed to have my family visit here? It took 35 minutes to get to the school. Would we grow weary of the twice-daily commute? I have moved a lot. I knew that sometimes what you love about a place can become one of its greatest downsides. I had loved the peace and quiet when we went to the lake. Would the seclusion be too lonely?

Located in the foothills of the Appalachians on more than 800 wooded acres, St. Bernard's campus is very appealing. However, most of the buildings are older, furnished with the parochial school furnishings I remembered in the '60s. During our visit, Kiki was bubbly. Before we even entered the school building she pulled me aside, "This is my kind of school. I can just feel it."

Brendan was much more subdued.

When we finished the official tour, the four of us drove to a pasture where two massive, white Percheron horses were grazing. Watching the beautiful creatures, I wanted to know that this choice was going to be positive for Brendan and Kiki. Things were so good for them in Chapel Hill. Did it really make sense to rock the boat? What about me? Our life in Chapel Hill was good for me too. Standing on the precipice of choice, I wanted to know that no one would fall. Leaning over the wooden fence and staring at those majestic, unbridled horses, I thought the choice in front of us felt no smaller than these massive creatures. Although much was in the balance, I felt strong, centered.

Malcolm and I decided we were not going to leave Chapel Hill unless it was a unanimous "yes." Since this was a move of choice, we didn't need to be dragging angry teenagers to Alabama. I knew the kids had had enough unwanted change; I wasn't going to inflict any more. Malcolm's excitement about the possibility of bringing us to the home he loved was tempered by his awareness that leaving North Carolina would mean I would be saying good-bye to amazing friends, my business, my church, and a lifestyle that I loved.

After touring the school, the four of us went to Dairy Queen and took stock. We talked about what we could do to make a move as easy as possible. We tried to foresee the potential pitfalls. Kiki was clear; this was an unmitigated "go" from her perspective.

"If this is what everyone else wants, I'll come," Brendan said.

Sensing the danger in moving forward with this passive response I reacted quickly, "No way, buddy. That's as good as a 'no' to me. I'm not bringing you here if you aren't clear. You don't need to know right now, but 'if it's what everyone else wants' is a setup for disaster."

Not expecting an immediate answer, we were surprised when he announced, "Actually, that football coach is nice and in a school this size, I might actually get some playing time. I like that we'd get so much one-on-one attention from the teachers. I'd miss Adam and my other friends, and I wish they had a better computer program here, but I think this could be pretty cool."

We spent the rest of the weekend waterskiing and swimming and looking at the lake house from a whole new perspective. The chambers of my heart were divided. One chamber was relieved that we would be together all the time as a family. Another was excited about creating an alternative, rural lifestyle. Another chamber worried about how Brendan and Kiki would do in their new environment, and the final one pumped a gnawing doubt, "how I could start over *again*?"

We spent the next three months preparing for the move from North Carolina to Alabama. Leaving was sad and hard. Van was returning to California. Living apart from their dad was going to be a new experience for Brendan and Kiki. Malcolm and I would have to adjust to reduced time alone.

One morning I slumped over the pictures I was packing and sobbed. I clutched the photograph of my neighbors, Terry, Susan, and Jane close to my chest. We looked ridiculous with our homemade "Ya-Ya Sisterhood" crowns and dramatic poses. Susan had given me the picture in a wooden frame with the word "friends" inscribed on the bottom. With the grainy wood pressing my palm, I rocked back and forth and prayed out loud, "Help me do this for my family." Then silently I thought, I don't have to lose myself this time.

Part Seven: Landing

"In the sweet territory of silence we touch the mystery. It's the place of reflection and contemplation, and it's the place where we can connect with the deep knowing, to the deep wisdom way."
—Angeles Arrien

Social Worker Wisdom

A few weeks before the move, Elinor and I were eating salads on the back porch in Chapel Hill. Long gone were our Project Compassion treks in the woods together. Busy schedules made it difficult to have time alone, and we were cherishing a rare lunch. However, rather than the usual laughter and jokes, this conversation was more somber. We felt the impending move as if it were a third member at the table.

"I'm not sure what I'm going to do once we get settled," I said. "What will my role be? Should I continue with coaching? Should I look for a job? It feels murky right now."

"What if you took a sabbatical?" Elinor asked.

"Sabbatical. You're the third person to mention this. Both Malcolm and Susan have said the same thing. I like the idea, but I'm not sure it makes sense."

"Why not?"

"Because I need to earn a living, and besides, what would I do all by myself in the middle of nowhere on a sabbatical?"

Elinor laughed and then she leaned in towards me, folded her hands and donned her "concerned social worker" look.

"Mary," she said, looking me straight in the eyes, "in the past six years you have moved three times, buried your best friend, started a nonprofit, divorced, maintained a multi-state relationship, remarried, started and left a new job, and started a new business. Stopping to catch your breath might not just be wise, it might be medically necessary. You are off the chart on the Holmes-Rahe Stress Scale!"

"What the hell is that?"

"Oh, I bet you've seen it before. It's that worksheet that assigns numerical values to stressful life events like moving, getting married. If you have a number over 150, you've got a significant chance of experiencing an illness. I'm just worried that if you keep going at the pace you've been going, your body is going to make you stop."

I thought Elinor was being overly dramatic; however that evening I wrote:

> *There is a yearning to pause, to create a stopping point, to change the rhythm of my life so that there is time to absorb the changes; to stop long enough to be enticed by the voice of . . . what? I don't even know. Wisdom? I know what has been propelling me forward—fear.*

On and off for the next few days I searched the Internet for articles about sabbaticals. My favorite was a story, told by Marguerite Stapleton of Sisters of Charity, about a South American tribe that goes on a long march. Day after day they walk, very quickly, until all of a sudden they come to a halt and camp for a couple of days before going farther.

A stranger, watching this, asks a tribesman why his people have stopped walking.

"We need the time of rest so that our souls can catch up with us," the tribesman replied.

Staring at the computer I suddenly knew: I want to give my soul time to catch up.

Continuing my sabbatical research, I revisited one of my favorite books, *Sabbath* by Wayne Muller. One morning I read, "Sabbath time can be a revolutionary challenge to the violence of overwork, mindless accumulation, and the endless multiplication of desires, responsibilities, and accomplishments. Sabbath is a way of being in time where we remember who we are, remember what we know, and taste the gifts of spirit and eternity."

Sure, I wanted to give my soul time to catch up and to remember who I was. But wasn't that a little selfish? Who wouldn't want all of that? Who was I to deserve it?
I brought the subject up to Malcolm.

"I'd like for you to take this time," he said. "I believe it'll make all the difference in the world. Brendan and Kiki are going to need you in a totally different way once we move. Think about it, this move is the beginning of our coming together under one roof as a family." His forehead furrowed, he took my hand and added, "Most of all, I'd like to see you give yourself a break. We'll figure out the money stuff. It'll work out."

Grappling with the idea of what I meant by "sabbatical," I decided to discontinue working with any of my clients after moving, and to forgo marketing my business until the end of the year. This would give me a five-month break. I still didn't know what I would do with that break, or how we'd make ends meet, but placing book ends around my time seemed like a good plan.

As our moving date approached, time in Chapel Hill slipped away too fast. The social schedule was chaotic, cramming in birthday parties for both kids, a surprise fiftieth celebration for Malcolm, going-away events, and my parents' fiftieth wedding anniversary party. I began winding down my business and felt sad about leaving what I had started. In the middle of all the normal "moving" mania, Van and I were re-negotiating our financial and visitation agreement. I was stressed-out and handled the meeting very badly, berating Van, attacking his attorney, and then feeling terrible shame about my behavior. By the time the moving truck arrived. I was spent. A new life? A sabbatical? Hell, I just wanted to crawl under a rock and sleep for a year.

Sabbatical Guide

After we moved to Alabama, the pace was considerably slower. Even though there were boxes to unpack and organizing to be done, we sprinkled our days with fun and settled into a comfortable routine with relative ease. Thoughts about sabbatical and what it would look like for me began coming up more and more.

Within a few weeks I set out to find a guide to light the way toward peace. At first I tried to go it alone, but soon I noticed that my days would slip away, spent on the telephone and unpacking boxes. I wasn't sure what it meant to be on sabbatical and I didn't want to squander this gift of time. A master at "doing" and a novice at "being," it became apparent that enlisting support in my desire for renewal would be wise. The starting point for my guide search was to revisit the Benedictine sisters at Sacred Heart Monastery in Cullman, Alabama. The first time I went to the monastery had been early in my relationship with Malcolm. He wanted me to see where he had facilitated an annual retreat for people living with HIV/AIDS. On that initial visit I was enchanted by the peaceful grounds and the deeply spiritual women who lived there.

One morning after I dropped Brendan and Kiki off at school, I stopped by to check out the monastery's retreat schedule. Driving into the long, circular driveway, I felt welcomed by the tall, white statue of Jesus, arms outstretched at the center of the circle. Large shade trees adorned both sides of the driveway, imitating Jesus with their outstretched branches. Small, contemplative gardens offered inviting statues, stone benches and tables. I parked my car and strode toward the monastery, a commanding red brick building with thick glass windows and massive archways. Once inside, I noticed the institutional flooring and dated furnishings—fitting for a mission that is committed to monasticism.

I found myself in the retreat center office and was welcomed by Sister Kathleen Christa (Sister KC) whom I had met with Malcolm on our previous visit. Sister KC greeted me warmly, surprising me with her recollection of our encounter more than a year before. Surrounded by her attentive presence, I realized how much I missed sitting with friends. Sister KC's loving manner was a balm for my unacknowledged loneliness. She inquired about the move and quietly listened as I shared my desire to find a spiritual mentor to assist me during my sabbatical. I told her that I had been sporadically practicing the Christian contemplative practice called centering prayer, and wanted to find a teacher. After asking clarifying questions, she leaned forward and patted my arm.

"Sister Mary would be good for you. She's very involved in centering prayer—she actually helped start the centering prayer movement in Birmingham. Also, after her bout with breast cancer, she became a massage therapist and does healing touch. She's really quite good at it—I love it."

Sister KC paused, "Yes, I think she'd be a great fit for you since she has studied other traditions as well. Here, I'll write down her number. She's available for phone calls from 8:00–9:00 each morning."

Speaking to Sister Mary on the telephone the next morning, I was disappointed that she couldn't see me for several weeks. I thought her tone was abrupt, and I wasn't sure she and I would be such a good match. When the day of our appointment finally came, I returned to the monastery and walked down a metal flight of steps to Sister Mary's office in the basement. Holding the cold, steel railing I glanced at an array of magazines and books resting on the landing at the bottom of the steps. When I saw Thich Nhat Hanh's *Being Peace* and the Dalai Lama's *The Art of Happiness,* I was pleasantly surprised by the diverse selection. Sister Mary's white door was open just a crack. Scented candles and soothing music wafted into the hallway. I gently knocked on the door and was answered by a robust, "Come in, come in."

Seated behind her desk was a tall woman with short gray hair accented with tufts of snowy white. Her small, hazel eyes shone as her round, red cheeks deepened into a smile. She looked like a cross between Mother Teresa and Mrs. Claus—sans wrinkles and round belly. Approaching her desk I noticed piles of books. At the top of one of the piles was a large blue book that had an illustration of open hands with rays of light coming from them. I hadn't seen this book in years—it was a book I had bought for Rhonda; one that had been used by an energy healer Rhonda and I had both visited. What was this sister doing with Barbara Brennan's *Hands of Light: A Guide to Healing through the Human Energy Field*? This woman was not of the same ilk as those strict, ruler-wielding nuns who taught me decades ago at Our Lady of Peace Elementary School.

Sister Mary walked over and closed the door, then motioned me toward a corner of the room and two comfortable chairs. We sat facing each other in that awkward moment of not yet knowing one another. Unable to hold her gaze, I dropped my eyes off to the right, a low ledge with candles, crosses, and beautiful artwork perched on it.

"How about if we close our eyes and take a moment to center?" she asked.

Folding my hands on my lap, I closed my eyes and returned to the familiar place of equanimity that can come from silence. After awhile, I peeked to see if Sister Mary was waiting for me. She was not. I closed my eyes again.

"Come, breath of God," she unexpectedly asked, and then followed with a comforting prayer. Soon afterwards we both opened our eyes.

I looked at her and smiled. I felt softer. She looked even softer. We spent the next two hours together, at first talking and then moving to a small adjoining area where I received healing touch and a light massage. Sister Mary knew about healing and she knew about "being with" God. Having taken sabbaticals herself, she understood the pleasures and pitfalls of time away from routine. When I lamented that I didn't know what I was supposed to do during my time off she gave one of her hearty, "ho, ho" laughs.

"I understand. That can be one of the most challenging parts of a sabbatical," she said. "It's really about just being, but if you're looking for something specific, I do have some ideas I think will help."

I grabbed my purple suede journal and opened to the page where a pen rested. I scribed Mary's suggestions.

"While on sabbatical take time every day for these things," she said.

"First, *rest*. Sleep. You are *not* in charge of the universe or even your own life. Sit in silence with God."

I scribbled furiously.

"Second, open your senses and notice all the gifts of life around you. *Praise* and acknowledge this is good!"

I loved what I was hearing.

"Third, feed yourself with creative time. And finally, live in wonder and awe at the magnitude of God's creation."

I circled the words *rest*, *sit*, *praise*, *creative*, *wonder*, and *awe*. Then I looked up at Sister Mary. "This feels doable. It helps just to have some kind of guidelines to remind me what this time is about."

"Good. Most importantly, you need to allow enough quiet time with God to give her the opportunity to take your face between her hands, turn your head and say, 'Over here! Look over here, Mary!'"

I stopped writing and we both relaxed back in our chairs. Mine was one of those comfortable old, upholstered rocking chairs. Rocking back and forth and grinning at Sister Mary, I felt hope seeping into me like rainwater on drought-hard ground.

"Mary, whenever I've taken a sabbatical I've found that my perspective is dramatically altered in some way. The only way this can happen is for you to take the time to be quiet with God. It's usually very tempting to use this time to start big projects or save the world so that you can justify not working. Resist that temptation."

"I wish I knew what I was supposed to be doing with my life now that I'm living in this totally new place," I said. "I don't have any idea what I'm supposed to be doing here." Unexpected tears stung my eyes. How did hope drain out so fast?

"That's okay. God is growing you," she smiled and nodded. "Trust that God is growing you." I could trust that God was growing me; I just wanted to know if I was growing into a rose or a weed.

Consenting

Ironically, I approached my sabbatical days with the same tenacity I had summoned two years earlier while training for the marathon. Using Sister Mary's guidelines as a regimen, I attempted to create time each day for silence, praise, creativity, and wonder.

Centering prayer provided ballast. Sitting for twenty to thirty minutes became part of my morning ritual. When I first learned of centering prayer years earlier from my grief counselor, Carol, I was surprised that there was a Christian contemplative path. After years of sporadically practicing Eastern meditation, I started using centering prayer as my practice of choice. In centering prayer I found a marriage between "going home" to Christianity and being connected with Eastern meditation practices.

Both the Tibetan and Vipassana meditation techniques I had tried in the past helped increase awareness of my thoughts and my attachment to those thoughts, but something had been missing for me. The first time I heard the centering prayer instruction to "consent to God's presence and action within," I actually smashed the heel of my palm to my forehead and said, "That's what's been missing—God!" The daily reminder to open myself as a conduit for Wisdom to work through me was humbling, refreshing. This one act, "consenting to God's presence and action within," each morning served as a brief reminder that the Beloved was in-dwelling in me and reminded me to cultivate this Presence.

Frequently I would struggle with the word *God*. The distraction was a barrier. Finally, I began substituting, *Shekinah*, *Mother*, or *Beloved* for *God*. Later when I asked Rev. Cynthia Bourgeault, a leader in the centering prayer movement, whether

I was bastardizing the process, she assured me I was not. In a response similar to Ani Palmo's years before, Rev. Bourgeault assured me the point was that I was inviting Divine Presence and action within me, not that I use the correct terminology.

For my birthday, Malcolm gave me a regal-looking purple and gold meditation cushion and zafu pillow. I created a sanctuary in front of a window in our bedroom. The window overlooked a hillside with trees and a small garden. Using an old chest as an altar, I positioned treasured items on the chest—a picture of Lama Norlha, a card from my sister Kathy with Jesus in the lotus position, a stone with the Tibetan mantra, "*Om mani padme hum*" painted on it, a statue of Mary from Mom, a handmade chalice from Kiki, and a jar of sand from Brendan. In the center of the altar was a tall candle I had owned for years—the glass was embedded with the figures of naked women standing in the "mountain" yoga pose, arms over their heads, breasts and hips prominent with touches of gold glitter adorning them.

Each day I would visit my sanctuary, read a passage from Nan Merrill's *Psalms for Praying* and adorn myself in Rafiki-like garb. Ceremoniously I would place my Tibetan Mala beads around my neck, then my homemade ceramic prayer beads on my wrist, and finally Rhonda's rosary beads resting in my hands. If I was in a period of discernment, I might include a crystal in a velvet purple pouch from Becky and rest it on the cushion nearby. Lighting the candle and incense, I would invite "God's presence and action within," and sit. While I sat, inevitably thousands of thoughts and feelings would arise—sometimes rather gently, other times quite offensively. Aware that I had been "grabbed," I would touch the thought/feeling with my sacred word—"love." On a good day, I might experience thirty seconds of true peace. Some days, my practice was unsettling and disturbing enough that I wanted to blow out the candle and run from the room. One time I envisioned smashing the candle through the window.

Other times, I would feel an overwhelming sense of

connection—to me, to the Sacred, to life... Over time I began feeling rooted and grounded. Centering prayer allowed me to be still long enough to give God the opportunity to turn my head and say, "Over here!"

***

As much as I thought I wanted this spacious time of solitude, having it was difficult at first. The powerful pull to maintain my habits of overwork, over-accumulation, and striving were well ingrained in my psyche. It seemed impossible for me to separate my self from my habitual busyness. Before I could "remember what I know, and taste the gifts of spirit and eternity," I needed to forget what I thought I was.

And then there was the daily life—the cleaning, folding laundry, driving, and cooking. How could I balance responsibilities around the house with my desire for meditation, prayer, painting, writing, and gardening? At first, I appreciated being able to tend to these tasks during the day, which allowed for more relaxed family time at night. But over time, I resented my choice to allow my sabbatical to be "eaten up" by mundane jobs. I gave myself pep talks about lowering my standards around the house in order to free up time.

"It's okay if the floor is dirty, no one stops by anyway."

"People who love you will love you whether your home is dirty or clean."

"Remember how Mom drove you crazy with her need for clean? You won't be doing that to Brendan and Kiki."

The first time I pulled out the canvas and paints, all I noticed was the dog hair covering the carpet. How could I paint for pleasure when the house was a mess?

When Malcolm and the children were home in the evening, I took on the role of doing everything because I felt their days were busier than mine, their activities more important. Even when they offered to help, I would shoo them away with a "No, no, it's okay." One morning after my centering prayer, a "flash" ran across my brain. *You believe that someone not working for pay outside the home needs to maintain impeccable standards within the home. You believe work without pay is not valuable.*

That night Malcolm and I were sipping red wine on the deck and listening to a chorus of tree frogs. I shared my earlier realization.

"I've got something I want you to hear loud and clear," he said. "I do not expect this house to be spotless or for there to be a great meal on the table every night." Resting his elbows on his knees and inching toward the end of his chair, Malcolm almost seemed irritated. "I not only support you taking time for creativity and prayer, if that's what you want, I want it for you. These opportunities don't come around very often in life. I want you to use this time in a way that feeds you."

"It just seems wrong for you to work so hard all day and the kids to be busy at school and for me to expect you to help around here when I've been home all day. I'm not even making any money." I whined.

"It's okay. We're gonna have to do more around the house when you start working again anyway. Besides, you underestimate the value of what you do around here—the grocery shopping, laundry, cooking, being present for Brendan and Kiki after school. I'm convinced one of the reasons this move has gone so well for everyone is because of the millions of little things you do that go unnoticed. More importantly, I see you smiling more often. You're enjoying life differently than before. That has brought joy into all of our lives. Haven't you noticed all the laughter in this house lately?"

Malcolm leaned over and kissed the top of my forehead. "I don't resent a thing—this is the life I've always wanted. This is the family I've always wanted."

"Yeah," I said, "you've really won the lottery! Let's see, you've got a non-income producing, peri-menopausal wife, hormonal teenagers, a cat you are allergic to, and two huge labs that are ruining your wood floors. You sure are a lucky guy!"

Although I had been kidding, for the most part, I couldn't help but wonder: if Malcolm could value me and my time in this way, why can't I? We agreed to give this new way, reduced housework expectations, a try. Until that moment, I hadn't realized that my slowing down would benefit those around me.

Even with our new arrangement, reduced standards didn't mean a total reprieve from household chores. At one point I asked myself, why do I feel that the time I spend cleaning, driving, and cooking is separate from my sabbatical experience? Could I adopt a sort of "chop wood, carry water" mentality? One of my greatest hopes in taking time off was to strengthen my relationship with the Sacred. What is more sacred than my role as parent? Could I claim being a mom as sacred and holy?

A slight shift happened in me with this mini epiphany. I tried to see all activities in my day as sacred. It wasn't so much what I was doing, but how I was doing it. I wish I could say that I maintained this clarity most of the time. Honestly, on a good day, I remembered to be mindful only a small percentage of my waking hours, but it was more than ever before.

***

My visits with Sister Mary were monthly reminders to stay focused on the purpose of my sabbatical—rest, renewal, and questing. Before each of our visits, I would prepare a list of questions. One morning the questions in my journal were focused on my conflicted relationship with Jesus and Christianity.

I had been thinking about the labels we ascribe to religion. For example, much of Lama Norlha's message seemed more Christian to me than some of the post-Katrina "shoot the looters" rhetoric I heard on Alabama's Christian Right radio.

Whenever I heard Lama Norlha, he encouraged compassion toward those who had harmed us. He spoke of *karma*, not revenge, for the retribution of actions (*karma* simplified is the idea that what you sow, you shall reap), and that it is not for us to judge (let he among you who is without sin cast the first stone). It seemed as though Lama Norlha was more Christ-like than some Christians.

I took my concerns to my guide, Sister Mary.

"I really don't know who this guy Jesus is anyway," I said. "Besides, if following him means behaving in a way that I see some Christians behave, I don't want to be one. I do not want to be associated with people who make gay bashing, warmongering, and suppressing women a priority. Why don't those Christians care about people who don't have health insurance or the families that are torn up by war?"

The twinkle in Sister Mary's eyes and the smile on her face told me that she was not at all threatened by my challenge.

"Mary, why don't you read about 'this guy' and interpret who he is/was for yourself?"

"What do you mean?"

"It's simple. Read the Gospels—every day, a little at a time. Do you know about *lectio divina*?"

"Sure I've heard of it, but I don't know much about it. It's a way of reading sacred text and contemplating it, right?"

"Yep. Find out about it and use *lectio divina* to read the Gospels."

"I've never read much of the Bible."

"That's okay. This isn't for some theology test; this is for you, only you."

Prompted by Sister Mary's suggestion, I took time each morning to read one or two pages of the Gospels. Then I would sit with the words and reflect on them quietly and journal about what I read and how it impacted my life. One morning I flipped to the back of my journal and wrote, "Jesus is." After each reading I would add something to the list. I wrote words like humble, clear, focused, strong, determined, a leader, demanding, discerning, self-assured, unafraid, willing to be with the unacceptable, angry, a teacher, a miracle worker, compassionate, harsh, a healer, radical, loving, caring, and honest.

Over the course of a few months, I developed my own interpretation about who Jesus was. Malcolm was a knowledgeable resource, and honest about what he agreed and disagreed with, but respectful of my need to figure this out on my own. In time, I saw Jesus as a radical man who spoke to the needs of the poor and for justice. I believed he must have been incredibly charismatic to have created such a following. The Gospels told the story of a man of humility, love, and kindness as well as a man who would get angry and impatient with those who used their power to be self-serving and judgmental. I looked to him as a teacher who showed us how to allow our false selves die in order for our true selves to live.

After reading the Gospels I wrote in my journal, "What do I believe?" and filled pages with belief statements such as:

> *I believe that Jesus came to show us a more compassionate way of living and to change our relationship with God...to help us see God as Abba, a loving father...to allow direct communication with God rather than through Pharisees and priests...to show the path to personal transformation. Perhaps Jesus' greatest teachings are about forgiveness. I mean really, if the stories we have been told are true, this man asked God to forgive his persecutors while he was dying from the wounds they inflicted! It makes the forgiveness that I struggle with seem so petty. And maybe that's the point. Maybe it had to be so dramatic, so complete that we would be inspired, not shamed, into forgiving.*

I wrote until my journal was nearly full and my words had dried up. Then I remembered a series of mystical experiences I had had during the last Christmas season. One Saturday I had attended a women's retreat at my church in Chapel Hill. During our reflection time I sat on a large rock in the woods meditating when I "heard" a low voice repeat at least three times, "Your church is ready." I thought the message was scary and odd.

The next day during the church service I had an overwhelming desire to lie down and surrender at the bottom of the large, wooden cross. I closed my eyes in an attempt to hide from the powerless feeling. The only way to describe what happened next would be to call it a vision of some sort. I "saw" a vibrant Jesus with soft, brown hair and beard come toward me, his long, blue and white robes flowing behind him. He came directly to me, placing a hand on each cheek saying, "Do not worry. I will give you all that you need." Tears poured from me as I sat with my eyes closed, unable to understand what had happened.

Recalling this experience numerous times, I struggled to make sense of it. At first, I thought it meant I should go to seminary, but my attempts at finding a program that would be a good fit for my clearly non-traditional ways was fruitless. If I wasn't sure my theology made me a Christian, how could I enter school to lead a Christian congregation? I just wanted to find a way to bring people closer to God; I didn't have all the answers. Nine months after my vision here I was, perched in the loft, journal on my lap and reconsidering the incident. Finally, I penned, "I dedicate my life to the Creator, to serving others, and to providing for my family." When I wrote the next line, it felt unnatural, but honest. "I trust that Jesus will help me to have clarity about how best to do this." Perhaps this was one of those head-turning moments Sister Mary alluded to, a stepping stone on the path I had desired.

I didn't know why I had been such a reluctant Christian. I guess I had not felt an affinity to the doctrine of salvation because it excluded the likes of Yuka and Lama Norlha—not because they weren't Christlike, but because they didn't say the right words. However, I did want to act like Jesus—to be more loving, forgiving, generous, and wise. I wasn't sure if Jesus was the only way to heaven, but I was sure his was the path I wanted to follow. I believed with my whole heart that trying to live like Jesus would make me a more loving person, and hopefully, make the world just a little more loving. Did that make me a Christian?

The next time I met with Sister Mary, I confided about my concern for committing to Christianity and honoring other traditions.

"You need to know about Father Bede Griffiths. He was a Benedictine monk who lived in India. Father Bede was true to his Christian beliefs and he was immersed in Hindu culture. A maverick in interfaith dialogue, he spoke of Christ being active in the Hindu soul."

"I've never heard of him."

"Maybe you would like to learn more about him," Sister Mary said.

"I saw a video once where Father Bede held out his hand," Sister Mary held out her own hand and then she traced her thumb with her other hand. "He said this is Christianity." Then she traced her pointer finger. "This is Judaism." Tracing each finger she added, "Hinduism, Buddhism, and Islam." Dramatically pointing to her palm she declared, "This is God."

Driving away with the statue of Jesus in my rearview mirror, I chuckled at God's sense of humor, sending me to Cullman County Alabama, one of the few Catholic bastions in the south. Nearly twenty years after leaving the Catholic Church, I was being nursed back to spiritual health with the help of a Benedictine sister, while my children were being nurtured at a Benedictine High School.

Sabbath Walk

Grabbing the pink and purple leashes from the hook next to the garage door, I called, "Come on Daisy! Come on Boomer! Let's go for a walk!"

Nails scraping the wood floor, both dogs eagerly bounded

over and pushed past me, squeezing a collective 185 pounds of Labrador retriever through the door. I looped the leashes around my neck in case I needed them, but let the dogs run free as usual.

The leaves were beginning to turn and cool weather was a welcome relief from the blistering humidity of the past few weeks. I began pumping my arms in my daily ritual of walking. About half a mile into my walk I passed a pasture of cows behind a small, white farmhouse, home to a woman in her nineties who was born in that very building. Surrounding the house were forsythias, which bloomed in early spring, followed by azaleas and then a smattering of perennials that reappeared each summer, a legacy of years of meticulous gardening. In front of the pasture was a patch of tall, golden flowers that seemed to be smiling as they perched their daisy-like heads on their long, green bodies. As we approached the pasture, Boomer raced along the fence and one of the playful, brown calves kicked up his back legs, daring Boomer to follow.

Grateful for the gorgeous day, I whispered, “Thank you, God.”

My walks had become prayers in motion. Altering Thomas Keating’s teachings on the heartbeat prayer, I chose to say a mantra in time with my step rather than my heartbeat. As each foot met the pavement, I would say a word in the short mantra, “Lord, I give my life to you.” I have no idea why I chose this mantra; I think it chose me. Yes, the concept of surrender was becoming less frightening and more inviting, but *Lord* is actually one of my least favorite words for the Creator—it sounds so kingly, distant, and masculine. But there it was on every walk, “Lord, I give my life to you.” Not *Creator*, not *Spirit*, not *Shekinah*, but *Lord*. My attempts at changing the mantra were unsuccessful. Sort of like a child who has been put to bed and continually scampers down the stairs, this phrase kept reappearing. Eventually, I gave up controlling my walking prayer, even if it wasn’t behaving the way I wanted. Eventually, it became comfortable, meditative.

On these walks, I would hear Sister Mary's voice reminding me to "live in wonder and awe at the magnitude of God's creation" and "praise and acknowledge that this is good!" Her voice would urge me to notice the slightest changes in the temperature of the air; notice the shifting shapes in the clouds. This voice would snap me out of the past, away from the future, and into the now. Uncharacteristically, I didn't feel hemmed in by the routine of walking the same route each day. Rather, I treasured the miniscule differences that appeared in my surroundings: the lake rising and falling, the leaves turning from green to gold to brown, and the newborn calves losing their curly coats in their progression to becoming cows.

A friend once told me that when she and her partner first landed in the Amazon forest, their guide needed to point out the blue-headed parrots and golden macaws. However, within a couple of days of immersion in the abundance, their newly-trained eyes were able to spot the tiniest Amazon leaf toad. During my break from the routine, I understood the meaning of her experience.

Brush Strokes

A few years before my sabbatical, I had begun to explore painting with acrylics. I use the term *explore* liberally—my artistic abilities seem to have been frozen somewhere between the finger paint and paint-by-numbers stages. Once in Chapel Hill, I had bravely signed up for an art class with a gifted teacher. But after a couple of weeks, I quit. The other students were too talented, the class too intimidating. While the others were asking questions like, "When shadowing the profile of the face should I use…," I wanted to ask, "Is there any way to show movement in my stick figure so you can tell she is dancing on the top of that mountain?"

The truth is, I *love* painting—when no one is around. I love the way the brush feels against the canvas. I love the miracle of watching the birth of a newfangled color when two paints collide. Immersed in painting, I forget to be the person I want everyone to think I am.

One morning when I returned home from driving the kids to school, I dragged the easel and the paints downstairs and popped in a soothing CD. With Peter Kater's graceful fingers flying across the piano, I painted a visual representation of a short essay I had written, entitled "Stained Glass."

The thin, grainy, charcoal pencil left black marks on my finger and thumb as I outlined my vision of a white dove in stained glass. The charcoal made a grainy sound as it traced its way over each thread of the canvas. Like the excitement of a lover pressing an inviting kiss on my lips, anticipation quickens in me when the charcoal first caresses the canvas. After sketching a plan, I dipped the brush in the water, gently rolled it on a paper towel, and then swirled it in the blue and white paints. Hours passed unnoticed as the music and the colors swept me to a different universe—a universe void of language, void of time, void of thoughts, a universe of simple creation. My heart was light as I was engrossed in the smallest of details: Should the dove's head point right or left? Would the stained glass be better on the perimeter or as a background? Is this gold bright enough?

I didn't notice the shadows cast by the dropping sun or the ending of the music. I didn't realize I was painting in dim light until the silence was broken by Malcolm, Brendan, and Kiki bursting into the house—backpacks and gym bags in tow. Someone turned on the lights. Brendan and Kiki were kidding with each other. What a relief that they loved their new home and their new school! I walked into the kitchen to kiss Malcolm.

Kiki approached the easel.

"Did you paint this, Mom?"

"Yep, that would be mine," I whispered, now embarrassed that my creation was exposed. In the brighter light, the painting wasn't very good at all. My peaceful dove looked more like a military eagle.

"I love it! Can I hang it in my room?" Kiki begged.

"Are you serious?"
"Totally."

***

When I first left college and began a career in financial planning, I valued closing a big sale more than anything else. I'm not proud of it, but I tended to size people up based upon their net worth—it was practically part of the training. When my own financial picture changed dramatically, I was forced to re-evaluate my beliefs on an individual's worth. Even though I was no longer in a traditional family and my financial resources were significantly less, underneath it all I was still the same person. I didn't want to be valued as less than what I was before all of those changes.

During my sabbatical, when I was removed from the pressures of the daily grind, I was given the opportunity to tap into an even deeper well. I began to notice small, important details that had eluded me in the past—the many great acts within a day. I found myself considering before-unnoticed people who made my life better—the young man bagging my groceries and carrying them to the car for me, the woman with the curly blonde hair who delivered my mail. When I mentioned my observations to Susan, a friend in California, she remarked, "Don't you think it's like when you paint a picture? Each individual stroke may seem insignificant until you take a step back and see the picture, and then you realize the true value of each stroke to create the beauty of the work."

Unimpeded by the busyness of my former life, I began to see through new eyes and appreciate the sacredness of the strokes on the canvas of my life. Thankfully, stillness helped. Unfortunately, old habits hurt.

Peeling the Onion

Not all my days were peaceful. Sometimes I found my quiet time invaded by angry thoughts waiting to pounce. A favorite diversion from silence would be ruminating on an ugly incident from months earlier with Van and his attorney. I found myself reliving the incident during my walks and my centering prayer, bringing up renewed feelings of anger and shame. Why was I wasting my sabbatical thinking about this? Why did old stuff keep coming up? Not just with Van, but with others too.

Creating large blocks of undisturbed time left an opening for unfinished business to resurface. I had a new appreciation for the wonderful distractions of my long-lost days of busyness. It made sense that I had pushed myself at a frantic pace; stopping would have opened the door for honest introspection to waltz in. Some days I felt as if I was driving an emotional Maserati at 150 mph, no hands on the wheel. Having expected my time off to be bliss-filled, I hadn't anticipated the turmoil.

In preparation for a centering prayer retreat, I was reading Thomas Keating's book *Open Mind, Open Heart* when the term "divine psychotherapy" leaped off of the page at me. I read, "The psyche as well as the body has its way of evacuating material that is harmful to its health. The emotional junk in our unconscious emerges during prayer in the form of thoughts that have a certain urgency, energy, and emotional charge to them." A few pages later, "Simply putting up with them and not fighting them is the best way to release them."

How could I not fight them?

I remembered the insightful and difficult poem, "The Guest House" by the Sufi poet Rumi.

Guest House
This being human is a guest house.
Every morning a new arrival.
A joy, a depression, a meanness,
some momentary awareness comes
as an unexpected visitor.

Welcome and entertain them all!
Even if they're a crowd of sorrows,
who violently sweep your house
empty of its furniture,
still treat each guest honorably.
He may be clearing you out
for some new delight.
The dark thought, the shame, the malice,
meet them at the door laughing,
and invite them in.

Be grateful for whoever comes,
because each has been sent
as a guide from beyond.

Had all these years of trying to hide from my old anger been the jet fuel that propelled me during my busy life? Just as I walked away from the dark side of jobs and places, had I walked away thinking I could escape my own shadow? I wanted my soul to catch up with me, but anger found me first. Perhaps I needed time with one to get to the other.

Around this same time, I was strolling down our gravel driveway, leafing through the mail when I zeroed in on an interesting announcement. Beeson Divinity School's Lay Academy was offering a class titled "Forgiveness: God's and Ours" with Rev. Dr. Fisher Humphreys.

Malcolm walked out of the garage.

"Do you know Fisher Humphreys?" I asked.

"Sure, I've known Fisher for years," Malcolm said as he bent over the weedeater with a screwdriver. "He's a great teacher. You've met him and his wife Caroline at church. Actually, she's the woman you talked to for a long time last Sunday. I remember you liked her a lot. She has that striking long, gray hair—a fascinating woman."

"Fisher's teaching a class on forgiveness at the lay academy at Beeson. I'm thinking about taking it."

A few weeks later I walked into the classroom with tables shaped in a U. I was the first person to arrive. One by one, other women entered and finally a sixty-ish, tweed-clad Fisher strolled in—the only man in the room. He placed his books and notes in the middle of the table at the front of the class and greeted us with kind eyes behind round glasses.

"Thank you so much for being here," he said, as if we were honoring him with our presence. The class was small, and we were encouraged to ask questions and share our stories. I littered my handouts with notes. Many of Fisher's analogies helped me understand the essence of what I was trying to do in letting go of my anger.

"Forgiveness is not an event, but a process. It is like peeling layers from an onion," Fisher counseled.

Amen to that! I had been trying to convince my pious self that my onion was a shallot, rather than the monster-sized Vidalia it was.

"Forgiveness means suffering in a special sense....You are entitled to want to retaliate. It's only fair. An eye for an eye, a tooth for a tooth. That's justice. But it's not forgiveness."

Bending forward in my chair, I eagerly wanted to understand this wisdom. I could feel truth in the room, but I couldn't quite see it and touch it. I did know that a burning desire to get to some place of "equality" had kept me entangled in my anger toward Van.

"In forgiveness, you voluntarily embrace the pain of your own anger rather than expressing your anger by retaliating. You could say that you absorb your anger. You don't repress or deny it; you live into it, and you live through it, in such a way to drain the poison off of it."

This sounded like healing from grief to me. Even though I had tried to walk around and avoid it, I learned the only way to the other side of grief was trudging through it.

In the next class, I bolted upright when I heard Fisher say, "Forgiveness isn't fair."

What do you mean, forgiveness isn't fair? My brain flopped around like a hooked fish gasping for breath. I was reeled in by the desire to get even. I wanted to get even. The blood pumping double-time in my veins told me I was onto something here.

I spent days journaling about this "fairness" issue. One day I wrote, "Is forgiveness ever fair? If I continue to hold on to a need for there to be some balancing of accounts, am I not allowing myself to be held hostage by the pain?"

Committed to using my sabbatical time to learn more about forgiveness, I read many books on the topic. In *The Sermon on the Mount*, Emmett Fox teaches, "Setting others free means setting yourself free, because resentment is really a form of attachment.... When you hold resentment against anyone, you are bound to that person by a cosmic link, a real, though mental chain. The one person perhaps in the whole world whom you most dislike is the very one to whom you are attaching yourself by a hook that is stronger than steel."

I wanted to be set free.

Reading, journaling, and praying about forgiveness began to occupy significant blocks of my sabbatical time. One morning when Malcolm and I were reading the paper on the deck, I expressed my disappointment that I wasn't farther along the forgiveness road by now.

"What would it be like if you simply prayed for the intention to forgive?" Malcolm asked. "Sometimes jumping to the end is too big of a leap."

I really liked that idea of taking pressure off of myself and trusting that some higher power would know what to do with my struggle.

***

When we moved to Alabama, I had joined a book on tape club. Listening to the books made my 100 miles of driving each day more enjoyable. One morning, after dropping the kids off at school, I was listening to Ken Follett's book, *Whiteout,* and heard, "It is hardest to forgive those we have wronged." I pulled over.

Why had this line called to me? Why were there tears rolling down my cheeks? I stared out the window of the car at an empty, overgrown field. Left untended, there were more weeds than good pasture in the field. Just as the farmer let his field go wild, I had let the weeds of resentment grow in my heart. I had never fully accepted my part in the ending of my marriage to Van. The gnawing feeling in my gut told me it was time to peel another layer. My anger had been doing a good job of keeping the truth at bay—I hadn't loved fully; I hadn't been open-hearted and accepting of Van. I was a willing contributor to the end of my marriage. I hurt Van. I hurt Brendan and Kiki. I hurt myself. I was hurting my relationship with Malcolm by holding on to this past pain. How could I fully surrender to the love Malcolm was offering if I continued to hold on to this old, old, pain? How long would I ask Malcolm to wait for me to bring all of me into our marriage?

How could I forgive myself? When the wronged and the wrongdoer breathe as one, who says "I'm sorry" and who says "I forgive you?" Could I carry both of those? If I couldn't forgive myself, who could I forgive? In *Start Where You Are*, Pema Chodron reminds us that "compassion starts with making friends with ourselves, and particularly with our poisons—the messy areas."

I had spent a lifetime trying to look perfect. Messy areas weren't really a place I liked to hang out. Yet if I wanted to soften, I sensed I needed to first roll in the muck. Over the next few days, I continued to journal as honestly as I could about mistakes I had made—pain I had caused. It was hard, but there was no way around it; I had to walk through it.

Peace came in an unexpected way. One evening I met an old friend for dinner. She was driving through Birmingham and I couldn't wait to see her. My friend had been recently married and I was anxious to hear about her new life. As we sipped wine together I could tell she loved her husband deeply by the way her eyes lit up whenever she said his name. But soon I began to hear anger and resentment for his ex-wife surface. Over and over again, she complained about the way this woman constantly asked for more money and ignored their children. The amount of energy my friend was spending on what was wrong seemed disproportionate to all that was right. Listening to her irritated me. Why couldn't she be grateful, I wondered? So much in her life was good.

After we finished our drinks and said good-bye, I realized that what bothered me most was seeing myself in her. Like my friend, I too had much to be grateful for; I too spent time focusing on what wasn't right. I too had a loving, caring husband. Why couldn't I be grateful?

Unknowingly, my friend had given me a great gift—she held up a mirror I needed to stare into. I wrote in my journal, "I had the opportunity to listen to someone I love express her burden of resentment and hate; I wanted to apologize to anyone who had listened to mine. I'm sorry I wasted my breath and our precious time together on these unimportant matters. I'm thankful you cared enough to listen, but I will ask that of you no more. No. Ms. Resentment doesn't live here anymore. Her song isn't pretty anyway. Ms. Gratitude, she has a *lovely* voice."

Writing about my new attitude was much easier than living it. I was given the opportunity to put my new philosophy into action the next day when I walked in the door from driving the two-hour trek to get the kids to school and the phone rang. It was Kiki.

"Hey Mom, that new contraption Dr. Graham put in my mouth just came undone. I need to go back and have him fix it. Can you come and get me?"

"Oh, Kiki! I just got here. Can't you wait until I pick you up this afternoon?"

"Mooooom, I have a wire hanging out of my mouth."

"Okay, I'm sorry. I know this isn't your fault. I'll be there as soon as I can."

Speeding past the now-familiar farms, my brain traveled down a path so worn it had become a deep trench. What would it be like to be the parent who never had to interrupt her schedule to drive kids to unexpected appointments? I do everything, *Everything*. On and on and on and on....

This rant went on until I bored even myself with it. There was so much tension in my neck. I took a breath. How could I do this differently? How could I see this differently? I asked for guidance, for a path, a fresh perspective. I asked for a foothold out of this trench. Long car rides have their benefits.

Why did it even matter what anyone else did or didn't do? I had chosen this lifestyle. I had chosen to live far from the school. I had accepted the terms of the divorce agreement. This was me living the life I had chosen. Besides, couldn't I see that I was fortunate to have the flexibility to take care of Kiki without having to ask for time off? Couldn't I see I wasn't doing this alone? Malcolm was fully participating in all aspects of parenting. I had more support than I'd ever had in my life, and yet I was still choosing to be resentful of what I perceived Van wasn't doing. What a waste of energy. What a diminishment of Malcolm's contributions.

Then my thoughts turned to what it meant to have Kiki in my life—just this morning she kissed my cheek and whispered, "I love you, mama." I wouldn't want to be the parent who was far away from her. Being with the children more was what I had wanted from the beginning; now I had it. Me living the life I had chosen. I felt ashamed when I thought about how much Rhonda and Jill would have loved to have been alive to drive their children. My neck softened.

Pushing a Tracy Chapman CD into the stereo, I sang loudly

along with her, "If you knew that you would die today, saw the face of God and Love, would you change? …How bad how good does it need to get?"

When I reached the school, I walked into the office to sign Kiki out. She strolled in sheepishly.

"Well, young lady, you just couldn't wait until this afternoon to see me could you?" I grinned.

A relieved smile swept over her face.

Caroline's Gift

Thanks to frequent contact at church, I befriended Caroline Humphreys, Fisher's wife. Her companionship provided much-needed company. Because I often felt hemmed in by Southern culture, I especially appreciated her free-thinking ways. I could truly be myself with her. There were times early in our move to Alabama that I felt as much a foreigner as I did in Tokyo. With Caroline I could swear and laugh loudly without feeling self-conscious.

One afternoon she came to the lake for lunch. I told her that Fisher's class had opened me to many new insights on forgiveness. Caroline shared that she too had some old hurts she was reconciling. I was encouraged that someone whom I admired could be honest about "unpeeling the onion." Enjoying the sunny, cool fall day, we nibbled on quiche and shared our heartfelt desire to be better forgivers.

A few days after our luncheon I received an envelope from Caroline with a booklet and CD entitled "Forgiveness," published by the Contemplative Outreach Media Center. Along with Sister Mary, Caroline had been instrumental in the centering prayer movement in Birmingham. We shared a love of the contemplative. The booklet Caroline sent contained forty days of contemplative reading and simple forgiveness practices, a sort of forgiveness cookbook filled with healing recipes.

Each morning I read the exercises and incorporated them

in my day. On the fortieth day when I completed the booklet, I wrote, “It is an act of faith to forgive. Faith that we can do better; faith that letting go of the anger and hurt is more powerful than holding on to it.” I composed and sent an email to Van apologizing for the pain I had caused him. Then I penned this prayer,

A Prayer of Gratitude
For the stillness in my heart
I give thanks

For the light dancing on the waters
I give thanks

For the lessons of forgiveness
I give thanks

For the teachings on compassion
I give thanks

For the encouragement to be still
I give thanks

For the love that is in this home
I give thanks

For the beauty that surrounds us
I give thanks

For the time to search my soul
I give thanks

For the time to HEAL my soul
I give thanks

For the wisdom of those before for me
For the love of those around me

For the grace of every breath
For the fall of every tear

For the laughter and the joy
For the sacred space of quiet

I give thanks to you Creator
May your gifts to me be multiplied
With each person that I touch.
Amen

The Traveling Talking Stick

"We are all meeting in Asheville the weekend of May 12 to celebrate Kathy's fiftieth birthday," Dad called to tell me. I was shocked. It usually takes twelve months of planning to get all of my brothers and sisters in a room together.

"This is a big event—the first child to turn fifty," he said. "We have to recognize it. Oh and by the way, everyone said they can come except for you," Dad joked.

Later I found out he had given this same speech to all of my brothers and sisters. It was effective; seven out of the eight of us showed up. Of course I wanted to be there. I love being with my family, and Kathy deserved to be honored.

Like most families, mine can be a little messy. We have experienced the statistically accurate share of marriages ending in divorce. We have had to address many of the big life issues: alcoholism, homosexuality, pre-marital pregnancies, and more. I guess the bigger the family, the more opportunities for challenges, and the more opportunity for love. Even when we haven't always liked each other or the choices the other has made, there has been a strong foundation of love.

Mom and Dad planned to host a dinner for Kathy on Saturday evening; the rest of the weekend was unplanned. The women decided it was fitting to have a croning ceremony to recognize the first Krohn daughter's rite of passage. My sister, Anne, and I took the lead in "setting the intentions" for the women's circle and communicating with the others. Emails flew back and forth between my other sisters and me with jokes and planned surprises for Kathy. We decided that we would each speak from the heart to Kathy about how she had impacted us. In one of my emails I offered to bring my treasured Native American talking stick for the ceremony. I had given Rhonda the talking stick when she was in the hospital, and it had been returned to me as a keepsake after she died. I was clear this was not going to be a present. I even wrote to my other sisters, "I would love to use the talking stick in the circle, but I'm not giving this as a present to Kathy. It was Rhonda's and I need to keep it."

I had decided I was going to give Kathy a beautiful robe to adorn her during the ceremony. A few days before leaving for Asheville, I visited a local department store and was disappointed by the dowdy bathrobes. When Kiki and I left for the party, I still hadn't found a gift. During the long drive, I thought of giving Kathy the talking stick as a gift. I didn't want to give it to her because I felt I had to. I wanted to offer it from my heart. I wasn't sure I was ready to let it go. A pair of earrings, the rosary beads, and the talking stick were the only physical reminders I had left of Rhonda. Yet something in me kept coming back to giving Kathy the talking stick. Via cell phone, I sought advice from Malcolm and Anne. Both basic gave the same advice, "This one's up to you."

I questioned Kiki, looking for the voice of wisdom in my thirteen-year-old daughter.

"Kiki, what do you think? I thought I wanted to give Kathy a regal-looking robe for her birthday, but I haven't found anything nice. I'm thinking about giving her the talking stick that's on the back seat."

"Isn't that the one that Bill sent back to you after Rhonda died?"

"Yep. I'm really torn. I think Kathy would love it. It's the perfect gift for her since she's the one who introduced me to environmentalism in high school, when she used to read Mother Earth magazine. She loves Native American spirituality. In lots of ways Kathy has been a trailblazer for me. It would be cool to honor her with this gift. "

"Well, that sounds better than a robe, Mom."

"I know." Tears welled up in my eyes. "It's just that it was something I gave to Rhonda that came back to me. I don't think I'm ready to give it away. A part of me wants to hold on to the little bit that's left of her."

We drove in silence. Somewhere along I-40 from Knoxville to Asheville I remembered part of the poem "Epitaph," by Merritt Malloy, that Rhonda had chosen to have read at her funeral. It spoke to "giving away love" in memory of someone who has died. I thought of one line, "When you need me, put your arms around anyone and give them what you need to give to me."

I would like to say that in remembering this poem I had an epiphany and decided instantly to give Kathy the talking stick. I did not. I wasn't ready to let it go. Holding on to the hope of keeping my treasure, I dragged Kiki through the mall in Asheville looking for a silky robe. I couldn't find one. Scrounging through the racks, I knew this was not the right gift for her. Kiki and I walked to the car.

I was ready to believe that giving away the talking stick would be as much a gift to me as it would be to Kathy. Turning the key in the ignition I looked at Kiki, "I want to give Kathy the talking stick. It feels like it isn't mine to keep. It's time for me to let it go."

"You know, Mom, I thought that before, but I didn't want to say it."

The next day, an assortment of twelve lawn and folding chairs was arranged in a circle in Anne's backyard. Surrounded by a clear blue sky with a backdrop of pine trees, Kathy and Mom sat in two of the chairs, waiting for the ceremony to begin. It was an unseasonably cool May day. Kiki and I waited inside the house with the rest of women, giggling and smiling in anticipation of the croning ceremony. It was a powerful opportunity to gather. We walked out single-file with my sisters, Anne, Liz, and Maureen, our sister-in-law Marcy, and nieces Tiana, Leah, Tara, and Mina. We circled around Mom and Kathy and then each took our place in a chair.

Anne stepped forward and planted an iron garden staff into the ground in front of Kathy. The staff was decorated with ivy-like, iron leaves, and hanging from the hook was a small indigo glass candle holder. Bending over to light the candle, Anne said, "The light of this candle is a symbolic representation of the new light for this new time in your life as you enter your crone years." She smiled at Kathy.

Next, I stepped forward and presented Kathy with the talking stick. Looking directly into Kathy's soft, blue eyes, I felt a wave of emotions wash over me. It was difficult to talk. I swallowed and took a deep breath.

"Kathy, this talking stick has a history. It has traveled from east to west and back to the east again. Now it is yours. It is time for you to tell your story and to share your wisdom."

Kathy beamed a "thank you" and I walked back to my chair.

"It seems like there is something special about this stick that made it hard for you to part with it. What is it?"

I cried, surprised by her insight.

"It was Rhonda's."

"I thought so," Kathy said.

We passed the talking stick from woman to woman, sharing our stories, baring our love for Kathy; three generations of women from the ages of eight to seventy-three, speaking our truth.

Mom said, "Kathy, your father and I told you we loved you every day, even before you were born…."

"I have seen a lot of dysfunctional families," giggled seventeen-year-old Tiana. "I tell my friends all the time, 'My aunts are cool.'"

Kiki reminded Kathy that she was like a second mother to her when Kathy lived near us.

Liz, only thirteen months younger than Kathy, read a poem she had written especially for her, "Remembering Who We Are," which included the line, "The best time of all is when she remembers who she is. When the matron princess becomes the Queen."

Maureen, the youngest, held her newborn Josh over her shoulder in the soothing way mothers have held babies forever; gently rocking him up and down, murmuring sweet assurances, and patting his tiny bottom.

We laughed, we cried, we remembered our shared history. When it was time for Kathy to speak, she expressed deep love and gratitude. Legs crossed in her chair, Kathy reflected, "These last few years have been a whirlwind. I feel like I'm finally landing."

She turned the talking stick and I watched the light catch the feathers.

Her words could have been my own.

Part Eight: Healing

"God has not promised to take away our trials, but to help us to change our attitudes toward them. That is what holiness really is. In this life, happiness is rooted in our basic attitude toward reality."
—Thomas Keating

Broken Open

A month later, I thought I was returning to Asheville to accompany Malcolm as he facilitated a spiritual retreat at Kanuga Retreat Center. I thought I was going to see my sisters, Anne and Kathy. And I thought I was going to have some time in the mountains to play.

I thought wrong. I was going to Asheville to witness grace. In the two days I spent at Kanuga I found my heart broken open, exploding in fragments of love and admiration…over and over and over again.

Before our departure I was consumed with the details of preparing for our trip and getting the kids ready to spend three weeks with their dad. There would be 275 people living with HIV/AIDS coming to the retreat. Other than praying for them, I gave little thought to who I might encounter and how they might touch my heart. If anything, since I was facilitating a small break-out session, I had hoped that in some way I would provide insight for those who came to my workshop.

Arriving at Kanuga, I was nervous for Malcolm. He too had been consumed with details. After the retreat we were taking a couple of weeks off and he was inundated with the usual last-minute duties of getting out of the office. As a result, he was feeling a little scattered and unprepared for the five talks he would need to give over the course of the weekend. In a motherly way, I was worried about him. Soon after we checked in, I ferried him into the beautiful, small chapel to sit in silence and pray. Half-kidding, half-scolding, I said, "There is only one thing that can help you now—you better get down on your knees and pray."

My worries were completely unfounded. From the moment he started his first presentation, "When we have been hurt by others" until he delivered his sermon on Sunday morning, Malcolm connected—no, he fused with the participants.

Based on John Claypool's book about forgiveness, the theme of the retreat was "Mending the Heart." At one point Friday night, Malcolm invited us to share our stories of loss in groups of three or four. I partnered with two African American women from Mississippi. The first woman set the tone.

"My mama died when I was in my twenties. I was so sad. I just didn't expect it and I didn't handle it very well." The other woman and I listened intently and encouraged her to go on.

"I fell apart. I just fell into some hard times. It was too hard to feel, you know? I numbed myself with drugs. Just numbed myself. I'd come down and it would hurt so bad, I just had to get high again. I did that for years, you know?"

I didn't know. But I did know that I fell into a pretty dark place when I lost Rhonda.

"It took me a long time to straighten out. I thank the Lord I did. He got me through. He woke me up and helped me see I couldn't keep doin' like I was doin'. When I found out I was infected, I knew I wanted to make my life right. It's been hard, but I'm on the other side of it now."

I told about the loss of my first marriage. Both women seemed to understand the pain of a family splitting apart. Finally, the last woman in our group spoke.

"Eighteen years ago, the day after I came out of rehab, my nine-month-old baby died." And then she cried as if it had happened yesterday. We three mothers cried tears for her and for her baby. Before she was able to finish her story, the large group reconvened. It felt terrible to leave her without finishing her story, but she seemed calm as the large group discussion commenced. I sat in the front row next to these two women who came from such different backgrounds and life experiences than mine. I felt melded with them as if we were sisters. Somewhere in those ten minutes, barriers had broken down because our hearts were broken open. By risking shame and humiliation in telling difficult stories, we paved the way for our hearts to be connected.

Power of Story

Kanuga in June is heavenly. The crisp mountain air filled my greedy lungs with freshness. In the evenings, Malcolm and I walked around the small lake, gazing at the star-studded sky, entertained by the symphony of croaking bullfrogs.

Saturday morning, there was a brief Eucharist service outdoors overlooking the lake. During the "passing of the peace," the woman who lost her baby came bounding over to me and gave me a hearty embrace.

"I'm really sorry you didn't get to finish last night," I said. "I'd like to hear the rest if you want to tell me."

"You know, it's okay. It feels okay just the way it is."

I ran into her numerous times throughout the weekend, and every time, she graced me with a warm hug.

During the morning break, I sat by the lake and contemplated the profound stories of loss, pain, faith, and renewal that I had heard in such a short period of time. Similar to my experience with Project Compassion, I appreciated the healing that came not only from telling our own stories, but listening to others. Clearly the details of our stories were different, and yet there was a universal experience in being broken apart. Then I remembered an insight Kiki had shared with Malcolm and me on the way home from the airport from a cultural exchange and mission trip in Kenya.

"My favorite day was being at the orphanage with the kids in Nairobi," Kiki had said. "There were two six-year-olds that just glommed on to me, Anna, and Tabitha. They were so cute, if you just smiled at them, their whole bodies would light up. I realized they were very happy even though they had so much less than most

American kids do. When we gave them a bag of school supplies, you would've thought it was gold instead of pencils. It made me sad when they told me they were worried they'd get jumped by other kids who would want their supplies." Kiki continued with tears in her eyes. "Mom, I love them because I know their stories. I want to listen to other people's stories now because they taught me that everyone has a story."

Recently my beloved Sister KC had been experiencing difficulties with her health that required she discontinue working in the monastery's retreat center. Even though she missed her job, she used the extra time to pray and read. She had been reading *The Lemon Tree* by Sandy Tolan, a true story about an unlikely friendship that developed between an Arab and an Israeli who could have just as easily chosen to be enemies.

"We have to listen to each other's stories," Sister KC said, "and be willing to be changed by those stories."

It may be a divorce, or a diagnosis, or addiction, or the death of a beloved that shatters our hearts into pieces. But it is the desire to move forward in a different way that allows us to break open to the universal pain of others.

My companions at Kanuga reminded me that we are forever changed by our losses. I realized I had a choice. I could be bitter about that which is no longer. I could wear my pain like armor, deceiving myself into believing it would keep future losses at bay. Or I could create meaning from the pain and the loss and allow it to open me to life, love, and others in ways I could not have before. What my new friends were reminding me was that I could become free of the power my story had on my life.

There was still one area I wanted to address, and that was the harm I was causing by continuing to harbor resentment toward Van. My sabbatical had given me the space to heal most of that wound and the resentment had much less of a hold on me, yet there were still remnants of a victim mentality inhibiting me. Could I detach from my version of the story long enough to feel compassion and care for him? Truly it was time to fully open that blocked artery. I decided to consider what it would be like if I met Van for the first time here at Kanuga and heard his story.

Surely I would feel compassion for a man whose father had suddenly died when he was only thirteen years old. My heart could not stay cold to someone who cared for and lost his beloved sister to lymphoma when she was a young mother. If I were to meet him for the first time and learn of his heart being broken by a woman who no longer wanted to be married to him and how that meant he no longer saw his children every day, I would weep with him over this great loss. In distancing myself from my part in Van's story, I could better understand that he too was in pain. I could open my heart to him in a new way that honored him and set me free. It was time to release the final grip of resentment that constricted my heart. Having moved toward forgiveness for years, I wanted to stop working at it and start accepting it.

I walked from the lake to the classroom where my breakout session, "Sabbath Walk," was to be held. There were eight of us sitting on school chairs in a brightly-painted room. The door was open. Birds chirped during the silence and centering prayer.

"Does anyone here have a regular contemplative prayer or meditation practice?" I asked.

A middle-aged African American woman with a round, sweet face raised her hand and leaned forward. "I began to take quiet time to pray every day when I was incarcerated. It transformed my life," she said. Folding her hands on her light blue, cotton skirt, she relaxed into the back of her chair, and silently smiled a beautiful, angelic, peaceful smile. Humbled by her story, I was again appreciative of the importance of making space for the "wisdom of the group."

Later that day we gathered again in the large meeting room. Robin, one of the organizers of the retreat, approached one of the participants. He stood up slowly and immediately seemed to wobble too far to one side, nearly losing his balance. Robin steadied him on one side and he leaned into his cane on the other side. The short trek from the front row to the lectern was painfully slow. Holding on to Robin for support, the man shuffled, sliding one heavy foot at a time. We watched in torturous anticipation, hoping he wouldn't stumble.

Standing at the lectern, the man looked at us, smiled sheepishly, and then bent his head down to read. He began to read portions of Psalm 25. It was obvious that the man's ability to speak was impaired. Later I learned that he had suffered a brain lesion and stroke years ago. After the stroke, he had to completely relearn how to walk and talk. Now he was reading in front of almost three hundred people.

Like a record that was manually slowed down, out came the man's words—laborious and difficult to understand. However, we did comprehend the courage it took for this beautiful man to read in front of us. We all listened to his speech with nervous respect. He deliberately read:

Le-ead me in your tru-uth, and te-e-each me,
For y-y-you are the G-God of my salvation;
For you I wa-a-ait all the day long.

M-my eyes are e-e-ever toward the Lo-ord,
For he w-w-will pluck my feet out o-o-of the net.
T-t-turn to m-me and be gracious to me,
For I-I am lonely a-a-aand afflicted.

Exhaling loudly, the man looked up and beamed. A resounding standing ovation beamed back. His ability to overcome self-consciousness and fear reminded the rest of us to be brave as well. His disabilities were more obvious than most of ours, but this man reminded me that we all have challenges that can inhibit our ability to live fully. Next time I am afraid of taking a risk, I hope I will remember his courage.

I contemplated how easy it is to believe I'm different from other people. How could I could see myself as different from this man because I was not diagnosed with HIV or a severe disability? Yet I am one stroke away from shuffling when I walk. I realized how my natural inclination can be to believe that I am better than someone who would use drugs to ease his or her grief. Yet if I was honest with myself I would have to acknowledge I leaned on cigarettes, alcohol, and anger to dull my pain.

My experience with this courageous group of people taught me that we create labels to build walls based on our differences. Used as tools of separation, labels such as gay/straight, black/white, sick/healthy, Christian/Muslim, Latino/American, rich/poor, Democrat/Republican have been used for too long to serve as barriers to the truth that we are all human incarnations of the Divine. In the words of Nkosi Johnson, an eleven-year-old South African boy who was born with and died from AIDS, "We are all the same. We are not different from one another. We all belong to one family. We love and we laugh, we hurt and we cry, we live and we die."

Healing Services

Saturday night at Kanuga there was a healing service. Malcolm's message reminded us that we are all children of God. Reaching out to his temporary congregation—a congregation bound by a common illness, bound by a common stigma, bound by a common rejection from society, Malcolm leaned forward. His voice started out hushed and then built to a crescendo, as if he were saying, "This is big. Listen to me, now. Listen to me."

"You are a child of God. No one, *no one* can take that away from you. No minister. No teacher. No doctor. No disease. No judgmental family member. *No one* can take that away from you. It is a gift from God to *you*. It is up to you what you do with that gift, but *no one* can take it away from you!"

"Amen." "That's right." "Amen," the congregation

answered back.

We were invited to choose one of six prayer stations for hands-on healing. I chose to receive my blessing from Helen, an Episcopal priest from Mississippi with whom I had connected earlier. An impromptu conga line without dancing formed, as we placed our hands on the person in line in front of us. Linked by touching and being touched, we supported each other as we moved forward for our prayers, one at a time.

I stepped forward and Helen locked her blue-gray eyes with mine. She held my face in her hands.

"Mary, what would you like for us to pray for?"

"For me to get out of God's way."

Keeping her eyes set on mine, she prayed with fervor and conviction adding her own request to mine, "for Mary and her ministry with Malcolm, and for their family." With Helen's hands on my face and someone else's hands on my shoulders, I was cradled in safety.

At the end of the service a thin, but muscular woman in her late forties or early fifties with short, spiked hair and tattoos on her chest and arms approached Malcolm and me. I remembered her from lunch on the first day. I thought she seemed cool and aloof. There was nothing aloof about her when she came to talk to us after the healing service.

"I don't have much family anymore," she spilled out. Then she looked down and shifted uncomfortably from one foot to another, almost as if she were deciding if she wanted to finish what she had to say.

"I've pushed my family away. I have a past. I've done it all, been a prostitute, addicted to drugs…. This is the first time I ever had a pastor or minister not look down on or judge me."

At that moment in the push of the crowd, someone else grabbed Malcolm to talk to him. I looked at the woman, encouraging her to go on if she wanted.

"Reverend Malcolm is the first one to tell me I'm a child of

God."

My heart ached for her for all of those years of rejection and self-abuse.

That night, when we were lying in bed, I snuggled my head on Malcolm's shoulder and draped my arm over his chest. I was thinking about the woman.

"I admire her so much because she is working to turn her life around," I said. "I could see where it would seem easier to stay in a life of drugs and prostitution when no one had ever really loved you before. But here she is working hard to do it differently." Malcolm pulled me closer to him as I continued, "I've never had to fight any battle totally alone like she has. I have always had the love and support of my family. What would I have become without that tremendous gift? A gift that I completely took for granted."

The next time I saw the woman she came over to give me a big hug. I told her what I had said to Malcolm the night before and she gasped and clutched her hand to her chest. I was a little confused by her reaction.

"*No one* has ever told me they admire me before—*ever*," she whispered as tears rolled down her cheeks.

"Well, I do."

***

On the last day of the retreat I sat in the quaint chapel with light streaming through the stained glass behind the altar. Being in the beautiful church where our weekend had started, I felt a range of sentiments, from gratitude to sadness to peace. Malcolm was on the altar with the other clergy, waiting for the service to begin. He stood out in his simple black robe next to the ornate white and gold robes that the Episcopal priests wore.

A familiar wave of emotion washed over me as I looked at my husband in his clergy robes. I remembered being surprised by the lump in my throat the first time I had seen him in the pulpit offering a prayer. I don't know why it was emotional for me to see Malcolm in his robes. I did know it could be challenging to have the man with whom you share your life, your dreams, and your bed held up as a "man of God," because sometimes we place clergy on a pedestal. Perhaps one of the reasons I felt a tug when Malcolm was in his ministry role was that it was obvious to me he was where he truly belonged, in all his sacred humanness.

Malcolm began to tell the story of his older sister Marcy, who had been shuffled from one foster home to another until she was adopted by his parents when she was nine months old. In that moment, telling a story he had heard, that he had told, re-told, and lived his entire life, Malcolm choked up and couldn't continue. He looked out at the congregation, speechless, with tears in his eyes, and arms outstretched, his palms open. He smiled awkwardly. He looked so vulnerable I wanted to run into those open arms, but I sat quietly. My heart burst with love and admiration as Malcolm waited until words would return. As he resumed speaking, I resumed breathing.

Driving back from Asheville I wrote in my journal about all the people, surprises, and experiences of the weekend. Even though the retreat was entitled "Mending the Heart," I realized that I didn't want mine mended. I wanted to stay broken open. I want to feel pain when a mother cries about her lost child. I want my heart to overflow with love when I see Brendan shooting baskets or Kiki giggling with her friends. I want my heart to skip a beat when Malcolm pierces me with his blue eyes and smiles. I want to feel the passion of desire to correct injustices in this world. Our hearts aren't meant to be fenced off to let only the good feelings in. Our hearts require opening to pain in order to feel the depths of our passion and love. In this breaking open we offer ourselves in holy communion to one another.

Pinch-hitting Preacher Hits a Homerun

Our family tradition of "home church" was born out of the necessity to create driving-free days of Sabbath. Our worship leader changed with each "service," although Malcolm and I primarily filled this role. The service consisted of the leader setting a theme, choosing appropriate readings, and then time for reflection, discussion, and prayer. Once we held the service on the boat and used God's gifts of nature as a theme. Another time we congregated in the basement and forgiveness wasn't only explored, it was experienced in a touching way between Brendan and Kiki. Home church has provided some of my most moving worship experiences.

We also worship at the church Malcolm has been a member of in Birmingham, Baptist Church of the Covenant. I still struggled with labels like "Baptist," and missed my church in Chapel Hill deeply, but I became adept at reframing paternalistic or evangelical language that felt uncomfortable so I wouldn't miss out on the essence of the Covenant community, which was *love*. As a family, we split our time between home church, Covenant, and a local Episcopal church.

Covenant's pastor, Sarah Shelton, went on sabbatical. More than a year of planning had gone into preparing for her to leave her flock for the summer. Hearing different voices in the pulpit was difficult for some because they missed their beloved Sarah. I too missed her. However, there was something surprisingly invigorating about listening to new perspectives. For me, it was almost like showing up at my favorite restaurant to find that they've eliminated the chicken masaman with avocado I always order, only to discover that I love the spicy eggplant noodle bowl, too.

One Sunday, Rev. Rodney Franklin was Sarah's pinch-hitter. I had met Rodney a year before when he participated in an interfaith peace service to commemorate 9/11. Both then and now, I appreciated his humble delivery of effective words. This particular service emphasized prayer. Malcolm and I squeezed our intertwined hands as we sat in the pew, soaking up the mezzo-soprano soloist's rendition of the Lord's Prayer. I pressed close to him, finding comfort in the familiar feel of his leg next to mine, his hand holding mine. Kiki and Brendan were beside us, mustering as much respect as you can expect from teenagers in church.

Waiting for the soloist to be seated, Rodney approached the lectern, wrapping his arms around each side of the podium. He was wearing deep blue clerical robes with a melon-colored dress shirt and tie, which handsomely set off his dark brown skin.

"It is gooood to take time to be still with the Lord," Rodney intoned, extending "good" the length of two syllables. Then he reminded this temporarily shepherd-less flock that taking time away was important for the shepherd as well as beneficial for the flock. I liked where this was going already.

Rodney shared a story about a carpenter who was invited by a king to a banquet. On the way to the king's castle, the carpenter was distracted from the journey when he built a small shelter to house him in on the way. Then, thinking of all the ways he could improve his simple dwelling, the carpenter began to expand it, eventually building new, more elaborate homes, forgetting the purpose of his journey. Weary of waiting for the carpenter, the king sent another traveler, an "unbuilder," to help guide the carpenter to the king.

Listening to Rodney's story, I felt uncomfortable. Was I like the carpenter? Since my sabbatical, I had been struggling with which path to follow as I renewed my commitment to my work. Some days I would focus on facilitating workshops at the University of Alabama at Birmingham (UAB), other days developing inter-spiritual retreats, or coaching, or writing a book. As if that wasn't enough, I was researching master's degree programs and considering starting an inter-spiritual center to promote peace and tolerance. Leaning forward I grabbed a stubby pencil from the back of the next pew and began writing notes, as I was prone to do when hearing words too important to trust to mid-life memory.

"Let your desire to be with the King be greater than your

fear and insecurity," I wrote Rodney's words. "Even though you may not know the way, approach the journey with love and trust and know that there are many signs along the way to let you know if you are on the right or wrong path."

At the end of the service I approached Rodney and we embraced. "Thank you for your words today. I've taken two pages of notes. This is just what I needed to hear."

"Really?" He smiled, looking genuinely surprised.

"Really."

Weeding

Driving back from church, I looked over at Malcolm.

"I think Rodney's carpenter story and the wildflower garden are metaphors for the way I've been operating."

A year ago I had planted wildflowers beside our football-field-length driveway with great hopes for a scenic entrance to our home. However, I hadn't taken the time to prepare the soil properly and the contractor I hired was inexperienced at developing wildflower gardens of this magnitude. After a knowledgeable friend cautioned that I may grow more weeds than wildflowers, I visited the wildflower catalog website and realized we were shortcutting many important steps in the process. It was late in the planting season I could have waited another year to plant the garden. But I was determined to get the seeds in the ground by November and pressed on, ignoring the red flags along the way, spending scarce dollars to have the land excavated and irrigated.

In early spring, I anxiously awaited tiny green shoots of life. When the first poppy appeared in April, I stopped the car with a sudden jerk, the gravel spraying out from under our tires making a crunching noise. Each day on our way to school, Brendan and Kiki rolled their eyes good-naturedly as I clapped and screamed encouragement to my "babies." On our way home, we would cruise down the drive slowly to search for new blooms.

By May it was apparent that my friend was right. We had

more weeds than flowers. Discouraged with the results, I marched up the driveway one morning, sprayer and weed killer in hand. As I approached, a small flock of goldfinches flew off their perches on the orange and yellow Indian Paint Brush flowers. Butterflies flapped their iridescent blue wings, sucking nectar from the butterfly bushes. Determined to eradicate the flower-choking weeds, I lifted my sprayer, startling a number of grasshoppers and a toad. I looked around; my eyes opened to one precious life after another. It was as if a film that was covering my eyes was wiped away, revealing an exquisite world that had existed in front of me all along. I couldn't do it. I couldn't spray poison on that ecosystem. After a few minutes of silently observing the life that was teeming in the wildflower garden, I trudged back down the driveway, deciding to manually pull the weeds.

I spent countless hours hand-pulling weeds. Trying to beat the blazing sun, I would walk out to the garden early each morning, pushing my wheelbarrow up the steep slope. Slipping my hands into my scratchy, well-worn gardening gloves, I would yank them on tight, like a baseball player tugging on his batting gloves before stepping into the batter's box. Then I would systematically pull weed after weed after weed. I actually enjoyed it in a twisted, Zen-like way; the monotony of the task, seeing the small creatures, and getting better at identifying flowers from weeds, all added to my enjoyment. However, my two hands were no match for the weeds' rabbit-like multiplication. Every trip home as I drove past the weed/flower garden I was reminded of my misbegotten plan.

Farther down the drive was a completely different sight. Near the house I had planted two small perennial beds, which I had been cultivating slowly over the past two years. They looked more beautiful each season as I rotated potted plants from the deck and planted them in the ground. Roses, gardenias, azaleas, day lilies, Shasta daisies, and camellias bloomed during their allotted seasons offering fresh beauty each day. The beds were small and hand weeding was easy; they were near the hose, and watering was convenient.

"I'm thinking maybe the wildflowers are like all the different paths I've been pursuing lately," I said to Malcolm from the passenger seat. "I have lots of passions, but tending to all of them is more than I can manage. In fact, I can't be effective in any of them if I keep pursuing all of them. "

"I think I understand. Tell me what you mean."

"I'm wondering if I couldn't use the garden near the house as a visual for what I want to create in my life, that if I'm clear about staying close to my heart, I can trust in time it will yield something beautiful. Kind of like what Rodney said today about trusting, even if you don't know the way. "

I pulled out my notes from church. "I want to learn how to discern the difference between the king's castle and the carpenter's buildings. It's not always easy for me when everything seems like the castle." I said.

We drove in silence for awhile, Brendan and Kiki plugged into their ipods in the backseat.

"I think I'm just gonna let that weedflower garden be for now. It's beautiful in a funky kinda way. We'll know when the time is right to plant something new."

Wisdom's Dance

One morning during my prayer time I was completing an exercise in the book by Teresa A. Blythe called *50 Ways to Pray*. This particular activity instructed me to "bring all of your soul to and dialogue with Wisdom." During this "dialogue" I wrote, "Take a sabbatical-like day of silence, away from the phone and computer." Immediately I thought there was no way I could create that kind of space in my busy life., but I looked in my calendar and realized there were many things that could wait just one day, and those that couldn't, I could complete in silence. I vowed not to use my voice until my family came home that evening, and unplugged the phone and computer. I didn't even talk to Boomer and Daisy.

At first it was difficult to ignore the greedy computer's hissing temptation, "Come over here little girl and I'll open a whole new world to you." My resistance paid off; I painted for the first time in months—the back of a woman with outstretched hands and flowing, golden hair wearing a blue, white, and purple robe. I named it "Wisdom's Dance."

After painting, I curled up in a blue velour chair in the loft and spent an extended time with my journal, writing, "I have been wasting a lot of time figuring out how I can be solved. If I just start a non-profit, if I just get divorced, if I just make enough money, if I just move, if I just take a sabbatical, if I just finish this book, if I just get my Divinity degree…everything will be okay. What a pile of crap."

Pausing for a moment I placed the pen in my mouth, considering my words and felt lighter, more playful. "Maybe I don't need to 'fix' me. Maybe I just want to be me. Maybe what brings my life meaning, what makes a difference in the world has less to do with what I do and more to do with how I am." Excited, I underlined my next lines, "Presence, cultivating a loving presence and making room for Wisdom's whisper to be heard."

Smiling I said out loud to the empty house, "That's it! That's it!" And then I thought, oops, no talking! I wrote, "Can I simply let go of the desire to be perfect and let 'me' be enough? I don't quite know how to start. Maybe being nakedly honest with me about what is truly most dear to me could be part of this new way. Maybe I could go even deeper with not worrying about what people will think?"

Journals are great receptacles for dramatic proclamations. I continued my impassioned writing. "If I want to dance freely like primitive woman and encourage others to do the same, I'm going to need to keep shedding the seductive fur of seeking acceptance. Who am I trying to fool anyway? God knows the naked truth about me…what I think…what I say…what I do. Why would I need to pretend for anyone else? Can I just trust being fully me will be enough?"

I walked down to our bedroom to my altar, inspired by a mystical sense of connection reminiscent of my sabbatical days, and lit my last incense stick. Swirling the stick in front of me, I broke into silent prayer. "Thank you for the love in this home. Bless all who come here." Walking into the kitchen I swirled the incense and unexpectedly felt overwhelming gratitude that brought tears to my eyes when I thought about Kiki's stories of orphans in Kenya, and how fortunate we were able to feed our children every day. I slowly moved through the entire house. When I reached the great room where our family gathers and retreats are held, I purposefully circled the area, giving thanks for all the loving moments and people who had graced our home, blessing those who would come in the future. Completing the spontaneous ceremony I bowed to the east, west, north, and south. If I knew how, I would have poured all of me out in gratitude and blessing to everything, everyone.

By the end of the day I felt a renewed connection to the Sacred and was humbly reminded of all the "remembering and forgetting" that I do; grateful for the illumination, aware it would be fleeting. I trusted I didn't have to grip this moment of clarity and try to make it last, because if this journey had taught me anything, it was that today's certainty is tomorrow's question. Inspiration is evolving and hopefully I am too.

One thing I did want to hold on to was a desire to keep my heart connected to the Divine Heart that, as Cynthia Bourgeault says, moves the sun and the moon. I hoped, perhaps unrealistically, to keep my heart broken open so mine would be a loving path. Just before Brendan and Kiki came home I wrote:

A Love Song to God

Breathing You in
Drinking Your cup
Singing Your praises
Is never enough

How can I offer
All of my soul?
How can I travel
The path of the whole?

Stay with me always
In dark times and light
Breathe in me Wisdom
More powerful than might.

Epilogue

Seven years have passed since Rhonda died. Recently Erin and Daniel came to play at the lake. Rhonda was right, even though they ache for her, they are loved by many. She would be proud of them. Erin is a kind, intelligent, young woman. She looks like Rhonda, but is very much her own person. Daniel is an athlete with a quick wit and a sensitive heart. It is always a gift to spend time with them.

One afternoon, I allowed Brendan, Kiki, Erin, and Daniel to take our small motorboat out alone while I worked in the loft. After a while I saw the boat come into view and I walked out to the deck, spying from afar on these elusive teenagers. I wasn't motivated by suspicion, but a desire to relish the rare opportunity to observe them in their natural, parent-free state.

Their laughter soared up to me like a hawk riding the wind. Brendan masterfully parked the boat and Daniel and Kiki jumped off to tie it up. One by one they launched from the dock screaming, tucked into "cannonball" position. I grinned as competitive Brendan wanted to know if he made the biggest splash. My sheer pleasure at being alive to observe this moment was nearly painful. I sensed the same intense presence of the Divine that occasionally appeared during centering prayer.

Who would've imagined that those four toddlers swinging on the swings in California would become these tall, athletic teenagers? Watching them immerse themselves in summertime joy, the word *resilience* rang in my head. In spite of all they had lost, they still embodied hope. Could it be because of what they had lost and survived and eventually gained that they welcomed hope? Once again I saw my children as my teachers.

I too had lost and gained much. The edge between "lost" and "gained" is thin indeed. Yes, I lost a beautiful friend when Rhonda died; *and* in her dying she gave me a renewed fervor to live my life like the precious commodity that it is. Yes, I lost a marriage to a good man, my children experienced deep pain as a result; *and* in choosing to walk away from convention and listen to my heart, I found myself and a new, more mature love. Yes, I lost a lot of money, *and* I learned to appreciate the gift that my family never went without a meal and always had a safe place to sleep. Yes, I lost my beloved Chapel Hill community, *and* I was given the gift of respite and solitude. So what is real in this tightrope between "lost" and "gained?"

As I look ahead to where my life may be leading, the unexpected turns in my past have taught me to be open to unimaginable possibilities—the mystery. Sometimes, when I struggle with where best to spend my energy, I think it would be easier to be "unconscious" about how to live. Yet, that would negate the beauty of those rare moments when the fruits of the practice come to bear and I experience the small moments—like watching the kids jumping into the lake—from a place of wakefulness. I hope as my life progresses I will be more grateful and less resentful, more loving and less selfish, and more connected to the Divine than the illusion of the worldly. And on those frequent moments when I forget all of that, I hope I can forgive myself for yet another human error.

I think of you often, Rhonda, especially when Erin and Daniel are near. Your being on this earth, it did matter. You touched many people deeply, not because of anything you did necessarily, but because of the way you loved. We are all given that same opportunity—to love with abandon and touch lives with the spark of our goodness. Even though you aren't physically with us, there is a whisper of you in our hearts, there is a whisper of you in the sun, there is a whisper of you in all that we do, there is a whisper and it touches everyone. Thank you, sweet friend. Shalom.

Acknowledgements
Creating this book was a community effort. I am grateful to the many who encouraged and advised me throughout this process. Three women served as literary midwives—Carol Henderson, Ellen Dossett, and Rebecca England. Carol patiently coached and coaxed this story out of me—reminding me to breathe when necessary. Whenever I was taking myself too seriously, she would sprinkle just enough New Jersey humor in our communications to remind me to enjoy the process. Carol's investment in this project is substantial and my gratitude immeasurable. Ellen Dosset's keen, kind observations of an early manuscript bolstered me to rework it; in the process I found what she had been looking for—more of my voice. Thank you, Ellen, for your tender honesty. Rebecca England's involvement goes well beyond the role of editor. Where the message was fuzzy, Rebecca would lead me down the path to clarity with crumbs of insightful questions. Our telephone conversations were peppered with theological discourse and holy laughter.

Erin Holman jumped in and offered to be my research assistant, providing more than asked for much quicker than seemed humanly possible.

Thank you to my parents, Margaret Mary and Dave Krohn—may I pass your legacy of love on to Brendan and Kiki and all who come my way.

A number of friends and family members took time to read excerpts, offering invaluable suggestions and feedback; you greatly influence my life and are present in the spirit of this book. Thank you for your belief in my dream and unceasing encouragement to my biological as well as sisters-of-the-heart, Kathy White, Liz Harrje, Anne Krohn, Maureen Hinchman, Susan Krohn, Marcy Marler, Jimmie Ruth Dodson, Patty Higgins, Carol Padgett, Caroline Humphreys, Mindy Gellin, Elinor Williams, Trish McDermott, Marti Rixon Smith, Karen White, Susan McCachren, Betty Craven, Sara Smith, Kelly Ross-Davis, Diane David, Tracy Clancy, Amy Lennox, Margie Powell, Sr. Kathleen Christa, Lori Bliss, Cathy Haven Howard, and Anne Cassity. How can one woman be graced with so many beautiful sisters?

Encouraging notes from my mom, Susan Jacob, Terry Randall, and Ina Durham were stashed in a file labeled “inspiration.” On the days when I needed to turbo-charge my shaky writer’s ego, I would re-read these notes and breathe in your support. What may have seemed a small gesture to you was a priceless gift to me.

If I ever needed a laugh I could always call my older brothers, Dave and Mike Krohn. My younger brother Patrick Krohn photographed the artwork and designed the layout for the cover. What fun to co-create with Pat.

Fisher Humphreys humbly offered guidance whenever asked. “What overarching theme will hold the book together?” was the first of many timely and wise questions.

Cathy Kiffney designed the ceramic work on the front cover; like all true artists, Cathy brings deep heart and soul to her work.

A word of thanks to my many spiritual teachers. I recall your words and smiles at the moments when I most need to find my compass—Lama Norlha, Ani Palmo, Ani Jamdron, Revs. Richard and Jill Edens, Rev. Sarah Shelton, Sr. Mary McGehee, and Rev. Cynthia Bourgeault.

A note to all of those inspiring souls who came forward to make Project Compassion a reality: One of my few disappointments in writing this book is that it is impossible to name all of you and all of the life-changing encounters with you—please know, you have my deepest gratitude. It is a blessing to see your work carry on.

In order for me to share my story, others’ stories were told, but from my limited perspective. Thanks to all of you, and especially to Bob and Anita Wise, who generously encouraged me to share a patchwork of the quilt of their daughter Rhonda’s story. You are both very dear to me.

How to find the words of appreciation for Malcolm, Brendan, and Kiki? Thank you for enduring the insanity of having a writer in the house with patience and more importantly, humor. Your love, encouragement and support provided me living water when my own well was dry. Your courage in allowing pieces of your stories to be told gave me freedom. As Malcolm and his buddy Rick are known to say, “These are the good ol’ days.” How I treasure the moments with you.

There are many authors and poets with whom I have spent much time reading and learning, especially Matthew Fox, Marcus Borg, Pema Chodron, Joan Chittester, Martha Beck, Barbara Brown Taylor, Wayne Muller, Lao Tzu, Rumi, Mary Oliver, Sue Monk Kidd, Rabbi Rami Shapiro, Roberta Bondi, and Cynthia Bourgeault; you shone a light on the dark path.

A profound thank-you to you, my unseen reader. It is you whom I have held in my heart in hopes that sharing my story would in some way nourish yours.

I hold the deepest gratitude for the Creator for each and every breath.

For information on Mary Bea Sullivan's retreats, spiritual direction, writing, or to purchase additional copies of *Dancing Naked Under the Moon: Uncovering the Wisdom Within,* please go to www.marybeasullivan.com. You may contact Mary directly at mary@marybeasullivan.com.

10-40% of all proceeds from *Dancing Naked Under the Moon: Uncovering the Wisdom Within* will go to nonprofit organizatons such as the Alabama Faith Council (www.alfaithcouncil.org) and Project Compassion (www.project-compassion.org).

Writing coach Carol Henderson may be reached at www.carolhenderson.net.

To contact Rebecca England for editing email rebecca.england@yahoo.com.

To view more of Cathy Kiffney's ceramic art work like that on the cover, go to www.cathykiffney.com.

Dancing Naked Under the Moon was printed by Images Plus at www.imagesprints.com.